A HOME OF OUR OWN

Gladys Ogden Dimock

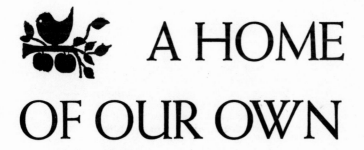 A HOME
OF OUR OWN

20969

THE MACMILLAN COMPANY, NEW YORK
COLLIER-MACMILLAN LTD., LONDON

© Gladys Ogden Dimock 1963

All rights reserved—no part of this
book may be reproduced in any form
without permission in writing from
the publisher, except by a reviewer
who wishes to quote brief passages in
connection with a review written for
inclusion in magazine or newspaper.

The Macmillan Company, New York
Collier-Macmillan Canada, Ltd., Galt, Ontario
Divisions of The Crowell-Collier Publishing Company

Library of Congress catalog card number: 63–9591

Printed in the United States of America

DESIGNED BY JOAN LAWS

Contents

LB
1782
D5

v

CHAPTER 1

Freedom to Starve

ON A COLD DAMP MORNING IN MARCH—A WEATHER SPECIALTY on the north shore of Chicago—I was in the small nursery off our bedroom in the dark little basement apartment which was the only accommodation post-war Evanston had been able to offer us. Our year-old son was in his playpen in the corner telling me he would just as soon be out of it. The language he used was private to the two of us and mingled with the sound of city traffic just beyond the windows that looked out on little but the feet of passersby.

I was starting to make up the crib when my professor husband came in, put his arms around me, and kissed me in a purposeful sort of way that conveyed the impression he had just made up his mind about something.

"I think," he said, "that you should have a chance to know what it's like to starve."

Though not prearranged, this was a signal. I knew at once what he meant and couldn't have been more pleased if he'd said he was taking me to some earthly paradise—which, in fact, is just what he was proposing to do. His announcement capped a series of discussions we'd had over the past several months:

1

Should we, or should we not, sever a permanent appointment at a large university in order to live full time on our Vermont farm, do some farming, write books, and be free?

Free from what? Not from earning a living, because our only income would be from writing. We had accumulated some savings and in addition our first textbook had recently been published but its capacity to produce royalties was as yet unknown. With this much financial uncertainty in the picture my husband's reference to starvation was clear. But didn't seem important.

We wanted to be free, I suppose, to be our own boss. We wanted to be rid of the demands on time and temper and nervous energy that an institution—be it academic, business, religious, charitable, or whatever else—makes on the men and women who work for it, who exchange their workday freedom for the security of a continuing place on a payroll.

An institution lives on borrowed time: time that is borrowed from its employees and is never paid back in the same coin. Meetings, conferences, telephone calls, coffee breaks, and just plain waiting—waiting for appointments, for elevators, for buses and subways, for the train home to the suburbs—minutes that add up to a large slice of a man's day. Then there is the daily drain on nervous energy, the battle with the insidious centrifugal forces that haunt the city and would tear a man to little bits if he failed to hang onto himself and protect the inner core that is the quick of the individual.

A professor is at least as subject to these demands and strains as any other worker for an institution. In addition to his teaching, his day includes a round of small, time-splintering chores not unlike those of a busy housewife and just about as stimulating. A meeting in the dean's office on a

2

matter of policy, a meeting with a colleague to discuss courses, a meeting with a student or, more likely, many students, to discuss their progress, sometimes their personal problems.

Meanwhile, nagging at the back of the professor's mind are the explorations among the mysteries and possible theories and unsolved problems, the fascinating issues in the field which, as a teacher, he "professes." These are the subjects of the research he will undertake or the books he will write "someday." But someday is seldom today, now, this morning, because it is hard to find enough time in one piece to collect his thoughts, think an issue through, and commit the results to paper. To collect his thoughts and put them on paper in a creative effort a man must be free. Not only that, but the freedom he enjoys must be of the sort that he himself would define as freedom; he must *feel* free.

Although both my husband and I have worked for many institutions—academic and otherwise—we are not organization people in the current sense of the term. For one thing, we are of the wrong generation, being today both in our fifties. Most young people seem to expect and even to hope to work for an institution, preferably a business corporation. Often, of course, there is no choice. By contrast, when we were starting out, the independent self-made man was still a national hero and the means by which he achieved this kind of success were more available than they are today.

In addition, my husband is a thoughtful man as well as the descendant of a Forty-niner, and I was raised on a farm and also in Europe where the tradition of individual independence hard won from feudal overlords lingers in the modern character. So we recognized the encroachments of the institution—even a benevolent one dedicated to furthering intel-

3

lectual endeavor—on our private lives and wanted to avoid or at least to neutralize their effect if we could.

Furthermore, it was not a retreat or an escape that we contemplated, nor were we attracted by the imagined and somewhat sentimentalized joys of the back-to-the-farm movement. Rather, we simply tried to figure out what kind of life appealed to us and concluded that it would have to be away from the city and the suburbs, in simple, clean, congenial surroundings. Hence the farm in Vermont, bought, as a matter of fact, more by instinct than by plan the summer we were married. And hence our long discussions—this time more by plan than by instinct—of the possibility of living and working there full time.

There had been only three major issues: What would be the effect of independence on our own financial security? On the education of the children? And on academic reputation? Apparently these questions had finally been resolved in my husband's mind on that gray morning in Evanston when, still smelling of shaving lotion, he came to the nursery to tell me about it.

This book, then, is the story of our eight years spent mainly on the farm, and what we learned about independence, about struggles with nature for survival, and about the joys of authorship, of privacy, of living on and eating the produce of our own land, and of being our own boss. One may wonder why a man with family obligations would want to give up a perfectly good job with an attractive salary and guaranteed tenure to sixty-five, and at the age of forty-three become a farmer and a free-lance writer when he has four children to educate and they, like their parents, show early signs of preferring the private colleges with their substantial drain on the

4

family budget. Of the four children, the three eldest were my husband's *du premier lit*, as the French have it. Living with us part of the time, and increasingly as time went on, they were beginning to be educationally expensive. There was twelve years difference between the youngest of them and Davis, the baby of the playpen.

Some might say that to make the decision we did at such a time was a crazy thing to do. Others might be more moderate and call it escapism plus luck. And still others—the number is not certain—might say, "This is what I myself have always wanted to do."

To us it didn't seem an especially bold move. Indeed, we'd been thinking about it for so long that it seemed the most natural thing in the world. Grown to boyhood ten years later, our youngest came close to expressing the real animus behind our move when, in a dreamy sort of way at the breakfast table one morning and apropos of some internal musing, he remarked,

"You know, it's *fun* to be free."

*   *   *

It was a short step from our decision in Evanston to the securing of a year's leave of absence from the university (the only form of hedging we thought of), to packing our belongings and furniture (here we burned our bridges, for we might have sublet the place for a year, just in case), to abandoning the shabby little flat to a retired vice-admiral and his family who were as glad to get it as we were to be rid of it, and transferring ourselves, our possessions, and our aspirations to the fresh green glories of a Vermont hill farm in May at the height of the season of apple blossoms and lilacs.

CHAPTER 2

Scrivelsby

WE CALL OUR FARM SCRIVELSBY BECAUSE THAT IS THE NAME
of the ancestral home in England for which we have a due
family feeling. Our Scrivelsby, however, has none of the glamor
of its namesake. It is not the home of the King's Champion,
nor does it have centuries of tradition behind it, nor are there
acres of sylvan park hard by Lincoln Forest with herds of deer
peacefully grazing among the oaks. Ours is just another hill
farm such as professors often seem to crave, with a brook running through it, an appealing view, two stands of sugar maple,
and enough good black soil under pastures and meadows to
provide rather handily for forty head of cattle. The house, says
legend, was being built at the time Lafayette was passing
through the neighboring town of Royalton in 1825. The
bricks for it were manufactured on the adjoining farm where
the plow still sometimes turns up similar bricks on the site
of the former kiln.

And the place has privacy. No neighbor house is in sight and
it is still an event when an unknown automobile passes by,

for ours is what Vermonters correctly call a back road. Also, the brook, which we have dammed to make a pond, has trout in it; but only when we stock it.

*   *   *

How we came to acquire Scrivelsby is an example of fortunate planlessness. I have heard it said that the Lord has a special deputy to look after preachers who drive automobiles, and I wonder if there isn't another to do the same job for professors in search of farms. It was in 1940, seven years prior to the decision made in the Evanston nursery, that we started our search. We had recently been married. The country was on the verge of war and my husband was an official in a wartime agency in Washington. On a rainy Decoration Day weekend we set out, our only guidelines being that we should own the place and not vice versa, and that it should be handy to good fishing. Exploring the White River valley pretty much at random in the pouring rain, we were cold and hungry when we came at midday to a small town called Bethel, squeezed in between a steep hill on one side and the railroad and the river on the other. The local hotel's hot soup revived us and we asked, as we had all morning, if anyone knew of a place for sale. The town clerk, we were told, probably did; he was interested in getting abandoned farms into the hands of solvent taxpayers. So after lunch we called on this official and found that, just as we did, he liked brick houses. He circled four places in red pencil on a geological survey map and handed it to my husband with the comment that in his experience the gift of such a map often resulted in a satisfied taxpayer.

At first, as we pushed through the rain on muddy, washed-out back roads, it looked as though, for us, the charm of the map might fail. The first place marked was a big, beautiful, shabby old house set in a grove of fine maples on a plateau overlooking the river, and in retrospect I wonder why we didn't stop. But we didn't. Today the house is gone and the maples have been cut for lumber. The second place was a small mansarded brick house set on a slope among a few big pines, with a quiet view of meadow and stream. We passed that one, too. From there the road quickly became worse as it wound up a little valley. Deep gullies appeared in the middle of it that the car could barely straddle. My husband is not a patient man under such circumstances, and he was driving. A certain tenseness began to develop between us.

At a crossroads there was an abandoned schoolhouse, some of its windows broken and the yard growing up to saplings. We turned left, crept along the edge of woods, straddled another deep gully, came finally to the top, and stopped abruptly in front of a brick and frame house on the right, surrounded by maples and elms and looking abandoned but, somehow, infinitely welcoming. We took this in in a matter of seconds. Then my husband leaned over and kissed me. We both knew that this was it. We got out to see what it looked like.

We pushed through rank grass, that had once been lawn, to stone steps at the front door, which wasn't locked. A high-ceilinged hall and a staircase were flanked by a pair of well-proportioned front rooms. Beyond the hall was a dining room and beyond that a big kitchen, its only furnishings a cast-iron cookstove, a broken chair, and a rusty sink. We explored further. The long frame tail of the house went on beyond the kitchen through two or three sheds, one of them containing

8

a dilapidated privy, and the whole ell topped by a series of bedrooms and attics.

The house seemed not to have been lived in for some time. In the ell, some of the main sills were evidently rotted and the floors shook as we walked on them. There were patches of broken plaster and stained wallpaper where the roof had leaked. Hardwood floors had buckled in the dampness. If ever there had been fireplaces, they were gone now. But there was a chimney at each end of the brick part of the house, another in the kitchen, and a fourth in one of the sheds. There was a smell of mice and a dry little carcass in the corner of a closet. A few pieces of furniture, including an upright piano in the parlor, seemed to emphasize the abandoned look of a house that has stood empty for some time.

But it was not its forsaken aspect nor its obvious need of tender loving care that attracted us. It was something else, and in retrospect I am inclined to feel (certainly not to think, because the brain has nothing to do with it) that the appeal came and still comes from some lingering spirit of the people who once lived there. The more we learned about them in later years the more a little lady called Mary stands out as a hard-pressed but independent housewife burdened by a large family with its share of tragedy, and harassed by a houseful of boarders and an eccentric, domineering husband no bigger than she but a lot noisier.

Mary had the sympathy of her neighbors (they once threatened to hang her husband if he didn't treat her better, and actually had the rope around his neck and over a tree limb when he promised to behave), the strength to stand up to her husband at least part of the time, and, apparently, the sturdiness to outlive him by several years of what must have been a deeply savored peace. Perhaps some of her independence and love of peace rubbed off onto her home, to be felt by us when we took it over. In any case, we and many others have noticed a certain quality, compounded of energy and quietness, that is intrinsic to the place, especially to the knoll behind the sheds on which later we built our study.

We finished exploring upstairs and down, looked into the cellar, which was full of water, stuck a knife into the beams we could reach without wading and found them solid, and then went out to see what the lay of the land was. Across the road to the left was a small gray unpainted cottage, and to the right was a huge gray unpainted barn. In Vermont, where a road runs through a homestead, a common arrangement is for the barn to stand directly across from the house, facilitating access in bad weather but blocking the view where there is one, and usually there is. But the man who built this barn evidently had an eye for the view, which spreads out below the shelf that the house stands on and rises again on the far side of the valley in a pattern of hills, woods, pastures, meadows, a country road, and two or three homesteads.

To the south, beyond the garden, the land rises gently through a pasture and along a brook to what was then a separate farm, the house and woods of which were part of the skyline. To the west, the shelf mounts more steeply through pasture and sugarbush. On the north is a windbreak of trees and undergrowth, and beyond that an apple orchard that we did not discover until a frosty moonlit night in October, several months after taking possession, when we walked out that way after supper and found an enchanted six acres.

The rain was still coming down as we got into the car and plowed our way through the mud back to town to find the owners of the farm, ask what they would take for it, and make a counteroffer. On the following day—one on which the sun shone bright and warm—the deal was concluded and we made a down payment. We would take possession in a month.

Late that afternoon we bought an appropriate bottle, drove back to what was now Scrivelsby, sat on the big stone doorstep flanked by ferns, drank a toast, and for luck, poured a libation on the step. Thus was ushered in a series of adventures to which, after more than twenty years, no end is yet in sight. All that a doorstep symbolizes in home, family, hearth, land, and community has become a reality to us.

* * *

Had the house remained as it was when we bought it we could have lived there quite happily for some time, prepared as we were to do without electricity, elaborate plumbing, and the so-called decorator wall colors. But as it happened, shortly after we took possession, most of the house burned down. On a Sunday afternoon in August a spark from a rubbish fire blew up under the old shingles on the roof of the ell. My husband and my eldest stepson Milton (a boy of twelve at the time) were excavating a new site for the privy out beyond the sheds when a neighbor's wife, coming into the yard, suddenly cried out,

"Oh! The house is on fire!"

Quite small at first—only a wisp of flame and smoke twisting up from the roof between two dormers—it was hard to reach, and having burned down among the rafters, it was stubborn. My husband fetched a ladder from nowhere (I didn't even know we had one) and an ax, and he and Milt climbed onto the roof while I grabbed a blanket, soaked it in the dishpan, and flung it up to them. But our only water in the house was a small flow delivered under mild gravity pressure from a half-inch pipe at the kitchen sink, and to wait for a pail to fill by that means made seconds seem like hours. When the pail was nearly full I grabbed it and ran out to the ladder.

"Oh, you can't do that!" cried our neighbor.

"The hell I can't!" I yelled back at her, and swarmed up the ladder with the pail in one hand, realizing at once that under normal circumstances she was perfectly right. Someone started bringing water in the dishpan from the brook, but the flames had gained headway in a fair breeze and to throw water on them from a dishpan was like spitting into a furnace. My husband got a lungful of smoke and had to come down from the roof; someone took the ladder away while Milt was still up there and he had to be rescued.

Neighbors had gathered quickly. The alarm had been phoned from a nearby farm and the operator had sent out the single long ring which on a party line, such as this is, means "Fire in your neighborhood!" and everyone responds who can. Neighbors brought out from the house what few belongings we had, including even the kitchen stove—a great black cast-iron affair. Four men clutching handfuls of grass as protection, picked it up, carried it across the kitchen, out the door, across the porch, and down the steps into the yard without upsetting a saucepan of stewing raspberries from which I had been about to make jam.

By the time the fire truck arrived, the frame tail of the house was almost consumed and the roof of the brick part was going up in high flames that reached across the road and licked at the big old maples beside the cottage. The firemen dropped a hose in the brook and concentrated on saving the brick walls. There was nothing more my husband and I could do so we sat in the middle of the vegetable garden, watched the firemen, and listened to the great rushing, roaring, crackling noise that is the dreadful sound of a house on fire. As the sheds collapsed, a high retaining wall that had supported them on the far side was revealed. It was a lovely piece of stone work and I began to visualize a flower garden there against it, with lilacs, hollyhocks and larkspur, peonies, sweet william, pinks, and columbine, in a perennial border. I mentioned this possibility to my husband, who nodded his approval.

"I wonder," he said after a while, "would people think me crazy if I hoed the beans?" At that point I could even laugh and said they probably would.

When the flames were pretty much under control my husband joined the firemen to see if there was anything he could do, and apparently there was. It was a hot day, they were all volunteers, and, well, a little something to slacken the thirst would be welcome. We searched through the piles of our belongings to see what we could find, and it turned out to be quite an assortment of potables, ranging from part of a gallon of red wine and some of my brother's hard cider, to the remains of a bottle of Bourbon and another of Mexican tequila. We set these at the corner of the fence by the road and although I rounded up a number of tumblers and jelly glasses, the more direct approach was favored, and so was sampling. Combined with the aftermath of stress, the result was quite a lot of good-natured nonsense and hilarity with which we were wholly in sympathy.

That afternoon we received five invitations from neighbors to move in with them until we could decide what to do, people we had never met and who, as we learned later, had planned to welcome us with a surprise party on the following day. But instead of accepting the invitations we decided to move into the cottage, which had once been an icehouse and contained two small rooms downstairs and two more upstairs. I found a broom and swept them out. Our gear was moved in by many hands. Someone made the bed and draped my husband's ties over the side of a mirror; the effect was almost cozy. The men set the cookstove up in the tiny kitchen, one of them went off to fetch a pair of tinshears to cut the stovepipe to fit the new location, the fire was remade, the raspberry jam began to stew again, my husband put a chicken on to fry, and Milt shelled a basket of peas. The firemen packed their gear, waved us a friendly goodbye, and drove off. The neighbors also said goodbye and went home to evening chores.

Left to ourselves, the three of us had our supper. After Milt had gone to bed my husband and I went out and walked around the still smoldering ruins that stood out against the summer night sky. Our beautiful house! To me the word stark will always mean a chimney rising against a night sky from the ruins of a burned-out house, a great upright against a broken roof, and everywhere the bitter smell of damp char.

The next day the insurance adjuster, summoned by our friend the town clerk in his capacity as company agent, came to view the remains.

"I don't want to worry you unduly," he said in a mild voice, "but have you read what it says here?" He pointed to the fine print in the policy. Of course we had not read it.

"It says," he explained gently, "that to build a bonfire in the yard invalidates the policy."

"But the fire wasn't in the yard," I said. "It was in the garden."

"In the policy," replied the adjuster, "a yard is defined as the area within one hundred feet of the house."

"This was more than a hundred feet from the house!" said my husband, rather urgently.

"Well," said the adjuster, "let's see." He took a roll of measuring tape from his car and we marked off the distance. Forty-two feet.

Fortunately for us it was a Vermont insurance company and the town clerk was our friend and interested in the town's business as well. He explained to his head office that we were city folk and could not be expected to know about rubbish fires in a yard, that we had had the place only a short time, and that if we were shown consideration we would doubtless rebuild and thereafter contribute loyally to the town's support. We got the money in full and rebuilt that fall. The restored house is smaller in the ell, simpler (no dining room), easier to care for than the original, and includes two fireplaces. There was no electricity, however, because the power lines didn't yet serve our neighborhood. And although plumbing was reduced to the barest minimum, at least it was inside and not out in the shed.

Meanwhile, another development—again, perhaps, traceable to the Lord's deputy in charge of professors on farms—turned our attention from the house to the land. Just before the fire a young neighbor had called on us and made us a proposition. He and his wife and two children lived on his father's farm in the valley, but so did a sister and her family and hence "things needed thinning out down there," as he put it. He would like to move into our cottage, use our barn, and work our land. He had no capital, however, and could not pay a formal rent.

This was a novel idea and, at first glance, not exactly a businesslike one. Nor had we thought as yet of restoring the farm. But it comprised about 135 acres almost equally divided between tillage, pasture, and forest. We knew that for years it had been considered one of the better farms in the community, that the barn would hold over a hundred tons of loose hay, and that a few years back the hay cut in any year had more than filled it. With this knowledge to guide us we accepted our neighbor's proposition. So one morning while we were still camping out in the cottage my husband found a piece of pencil, sharpened it with my paring knife (which I was never thereafter able to find), opened a grocery bag out flat (the only paper he could lay his hands on), and wrote a draft agreement which I later typed on the town clerk's machine. The neighbor was to occupy the cottage and pay no rent or share, but he was to operate the farm "in a husbandlike manner." Animals and equipment would belong to him, the land and buildings to us. We would pay for any materials needed to repair buildings and fences, and he would supply the labor. After our house was rebuilt that fall and we moved back into it, Richard transferred his family and his stock to our place and set to work.

Thus commenced the improvement of the land and barns over a period of time. In no year have we put more than $2000 into it, trying so far as possible to finance its rehabilitation out of the earnings of the farm itself. In the first three years both Richard and Scrivelsby did so well that when he went back to help his father on the home farm, we found someone else to take his place on the same terms. Indeed,

16

so encouraged were we with the whole arrangement that later, when the adjoining farm on the hill to the south of us came on the market, we bought it and since then have had a combined operation of thirty to forty head of dairy cows (we're part of the Boston milkshed) and 360 acres of land of which 100 acres are tillage, 70 acres in pasture, and the rest forest, including some fine stands of timber.

*   *   *

So this was Scrivelsby, the farm on which we proposed to invite our souls and our talents as farmers after a fashion and authors in earnest. True, despite the restoration, the house was still primitive in many ways. But what are deficiencies such as water pressure and electricity, we told ourselves, compared with the incomparable delights of living as we pleased, working hard all day on the land or in the study, and then sitting by an open fire of logs cut from our own forest, listening to the sound of the teakettle simmering on the stove in the adjoining kitchen, and savoring the good smells of fresh-baked bread and beef stew?

The odd thing is that it turned out pretty much as we expected it would.

CHAPTER 3

Settling In

ON A FINE MAY MORNING, A COUPLE OF MONTHS AFTER OUR decision to be free, we packed the car and I left Evanston with the baby and my second stepson, Mark. Davis was fifteen months old and had recently learned to walk. Mark was seventeen and was temporarily living with us. He would help with the driving. My husband was to stay behind to supervise the movers and finish the semester at the university. He would join us in three weeks. A rather battered black Oldsmobile sedan of doubtful antecedents (World War II had ended only the year before) and recently acquired from a used-car lot, was heavily loaded. The crib mattress on top of the pile provided a daytime bed for Davis.

Mark took Davis on his lap, I took the wheel, and my husband embraced us, with what misgivings I could imagine. Two days later we drove into the yard at the farm and even Davis seemed to share our sense of relief. I can still see him in corduroy overalls and a tweed jacket, running quickly and purposefully ahead of me to keep out from under my feet as I strode through the woodshed and into the kitchen, my arms loaded with gear. Mark made the fire in the kitchen stove and

18

unpacked the car while I looked after Davis, distributed the luggage, turned on the water, and made up the beds. We had a simple supper, considered the morrow, and turned in.

The following morning it was cold and damp in the kitchen (the house had been closed all winter) and it was raining. Making a fire in the wood-burning iron stove is a noisy routine that always succeeds in waking the family even if it doesn't get them up right away: shake the grates, remove the iron lids, lay paper, kindling, and small sticks, touch a match, replace the lids, set the drafts, dump the ashes into a bucket in the shed, and sweep the floor. Then check the drafts, add wood to the firebox, fill the teakettle at the sink, and set it on to boil. On this morning the shaking of the grates brought Mark downstairs and I got Davis dressed and prepared breakfast while Mark made a fire in the living room. The dampness in the house gradually disappeared but outside the rain kept right on.

I had just finished the dishes when the phone rang. It was the movers with the van. They were in Bethel. Where did we live and did I think their heavy trailer could be got over the back roads? It seemed unlikely on account of the rain, I said, but perhaps they'd better see for themselves. I would fetch them. Leaving Davis with Mark, I put on my husband's disreputable old rain coat (a dozen years later I am still not permitted to throw it away, though I do mend it periodically) and drove off, skidding and splashing through the mud. The Olds was not a "mudder" in the sense that a racehorse sometimes is.

The movers were both big men and having spent the night at a comfortable local inn (aided further, no doubt, by what Vermont's Ethan Allen was wont to call "the brimming bowl") they were cheery. But when they saw the wet little track that wound between the blacktop highway and our house they lost interest in it right away. They would have to transfer the load to a smaller truck, to be obtained locally.

The rest of the day was not one to remember if it could be forgotten, and I almost have. By the end of it the furniture was in, the movers were gone, the car (which had lost the use of its fuel pump at a crucial moment) was in the repair shop, and the house looked like the day before a country auction. By now we had been living in it during summer vacations for seven years and it contained plenty of furniture even before the van brought more. Consequently, on the following day, having retrieved the Olds, I sought out a used-furniture dealer and disposed of a load of things I thought I could bear to part with. It didn't occur to me that should our experiment fail, we might need them again. A big sofa upholstered in blue velvet with a hole burned in its back, bought at auction for three dollars the first year we were married, cost me a few sentimental regrets, but sofas were now redundant and I let the old friend go.

After that, Mark and I rearranged the furniture that was left and by evening, as we sat by the living-room fire after supper, we agreed that the house was comfortable. It was also attractive because there were some old family pieces that looked well against the gray, weathered boards from an old barn with which we had panelled the living room. There is a story that some of the first religious services in Bethel were held in a big barn on what, for that reason, came to be called Christian Hill. By extension, our whole neighborhood now goes by that name. The barn survived until the year we rebuilt after the fire and was being taken down just as we needed weathered boards. It was a fortunate juxtaposition of circumstances for us and we cherish our panelling as much for the legend as for the beauty of texture and color of our living room walls. These and the big pine beams in the ceiling are particularly effective at night; they were especially so in the days when we burned oil lamps, the light of which is soft if not exactly functional in other ways. But this night Mark and I were not reading; we were just plain tired and resting a bit before going to bed.

The fireplace in the living room is one of the two we installed after the fire. In searching for a mantel I had found an old hand-carved cherry bedstead and used the headboard in the living room and the footboard for the fireplace in the bedroom across the hall. And here is another legend: the bed, we were told, had been custom-made in France for one of President Lincoln's Secretaries, thought to be William H. Seward. The fact that in my salad days I had been in love with a Seward made this a rather poignant coincidence, but since Lincoln's Secretary of the Treasury, Salmon P. Chase, had relatives in our neighboring town of Royalton and went to school there for a while, we have thought it more likely that the bed was made for him rather than for Seward, and that it somehow found its way back to Royalton after Chase was done with it. In any case, the carving over the headboard includes a border of oak leaves and acorns and as the word "oak" occurs as a syllable in both my husband's last name and in mine, here is another happy conjuncture.

In our bedroom the fireplace is a luxury, of course, but in winter it is also a necessity since it is the only source of heat in there. Next to the bedroom is what for years after the rebuilding passed as a bathroom, though it contained only a toilet and a counter on which stood a full-blown pitcher-and-bowl set of Victorian china.

Upstairs the guest room looks out into the branches of an apple tree on the north and to green hills across the valley through a dormer in front. The slanting walls and ceiling in this room are panelled with pine and so is the hall, which is full of bookcases. The second room up there, which we used as a study until we built a new one, is panelled in seasoned yellow birch, a hard wood with a gleaming natural finish that shines in lamplight like satin. In this room also we had bookshelves and a huge desk designed by my husband and made out of plywood; it was arranged so that we could both work at it at once. The study could serve as dormitory also, however, and often did so as various members of our combined families came to visit us.

But it is the kitchen, I think, that has always been our favorite room in the house. For one thing, though sterilized by fire, it quickly regained a country-kitchen smell compounded of cupboards and their contents, woodsmoke, and the cooking of country fare including bread, the trying out of lard, and the boiling of gallons of maple sap to make a gallon of syrup. Since we have dispensed with a separate dining room, our kitchen takes the place of what in the modern home is often called the family room as distinguished from the living room, as though to congregate as a family were a function separate from living. Well, when the kitchen is full of family and I'm trying to get a meal on the table, I sometimes think there should be a difference. But for the most part our living room and kitchen and the functions thereof are pretty much of a blend.

This kitchen is panelled, countered, and cupboarded in

pine. Casement windows over an iron sink look out in summer on apple trees and a cool green lawn, and in winter on a pile of snow window-high. In winter, a form of self-torture (mixed with pride because you have learned to handle cold weather and know that in any case you can take it) is to check the temperature on the thermometer out there just before going to bed and again first thing in the morning.

Under the windows on the south side of the kitchen, the big harvest dining table is flanked by pine dressers filled with the old ironstone china that we not only collect but use. Beyond is the garden, the pond (produced from the brook by a Soil Conservation Service bulldozer), and the pasture that rises along the brook to the trees on the horizon. In summer this pasture is the usual uneven, rocky terrain typical of a hill farm in Vermont, but in winter deep snows cover the craggyness, the rocks, the tufts of hardhack and juniper, even the fences. The smooth, gently undulating surface shines in the sunlight, especially after a crust has formed on the snow, and ice crystals sparkle against a deep blue sky. This white-and-gold-and-blue effect is something for which a body could live, like the first day of spring. No summer visitor to the north country ever sees it—and such a pity.

The central feature of the kitchen, standing square against the side wall, was a great cast-iron wood-burning cookstove, an Andes. It was the same that made the journey to the cottage after the fire, and back again on my husband's birthday, which was when we first reoccupied the restored house. A high warming shelf that hugged the stovepipe, and two smaller ones lower down on the sides, gave that monster an odd look of stretching out its arms to you. But this was deceptive. It could also sulk in a morose fit of introspection.

Temperamental as to drafts and diet, it responded in an almost human way to the mood of its handler. It was a glutton for wood and, if I really pushed it with rock maple, would glow a deep angry red on its iron top. At other times it was just plain ornery and nothing could persuade it to warm the oven, a cavernous affair designed to take the biggest turkey a farm family could offer it or to bake a week's supply of bread.

If the wind was from the northwest (which fortunately isn't often), this big black devil would sit there against the wall and repeatedly belch forth thick smoke from every crack and cranny as each gust struck the chimney, and we'd have to open windows and doors to clear the air. In winter, with the outside temperature at zero or under, this was a problem and we had to let the smoke gradually dissipate into the upper regions of the house while we went about in the meantime with streaming eyes.

This stove required loving care as a matter of routine. Its ashes had to be disposed of each morning, and once every few weeks its pipes and insides had to be cleaned of ashes and soot. This meant virtually taking it apart, removing all the lids and top frames, scraping out the between-decks areas under and over the oven, disconnecting the stovepipe, taking it carefully to the yard, dumping the accumulation of soot, and burning out the remaining creosote with kerosene. Then everything had to be wiped clean and put back together again. But when the job was done and the whole of the monster's big black body had been polished with a black liquid that is indelible on the hands, he would sit there and smile at his beholder in a smug, self-satisfied, but wholly irresistible way.

Although it may not be scientifically demonstrable, I have heard it said and do believe it, that heat derived from wood has a different quality from that derived from oil, gas, or electricity. Wood heat *feels* different; it is a more comfortable, a more friendly heat. A neighbor said to me recently that he had been hoping for years to save enough money to install a furnace, but that if he ever did he'd still keep a chunk stove around just for the comfort of its special kind of heat. As for cooking, when I bake or roast in this oven, the food has a better flavor and even a better texture than that which is cooked in a gas oven. In addition, the spatter of fat, which is a problem in a modern range oven, seems merely to burn off in a wood-burner.

I have also learned the advantages of cooking over a diffused rather than a spot heat: the pan can be moved from a rolling boil or a fast fry to a gentle simmer or a sauté according to its distance from the area immediately over the firebox. Furthermore, in a wood-burner a constant fire means that all parts of the stove can be used at any time without special attention to lighting and pre-heating the oven, for example, and without remembering that the fuel is metered. A pot of stew can simmer on the back of the stove all day and all night too without burning extra wood, and at a gentle temperature that is impossible (despite the salesman's oratory) with a spot burner. Oatmeal cooked gently overnight is a taste adventure that many city folk have never known.

Perhaps the masterpiece of cookery on a wood-burner is broiling meat. Instead of heating a steak from the top and forcing the juices out, you place it on a wire rack over live coals and turn it when the juices start to drip, thus heading them back into the meat. And then there is the fine, compelling odor of broiling steak or lamb chops or chicken. Perhaps one reason for the current popularity of cookouts (that symbol of American togetherness) in the suburban backyard is that meat is so much tastier when cooked over coals instead of under a nice clean gas or electric grid.

To me, for all of these reasons, that wood-burner was friend, fiend, and challenge. It was also the only source of heat in that part of the house, and I learned to make it purr. When it finally rusted out in strategic spots that could not be repaired, we sold it for junk; it cost me something to watch the junkman destroy it with a sledge hammer before loading it on his truck. Its successor, younger by maybe thirty years and called a Home Comfort, is leaner and better disciplined, but less interesting.

Despite the rebuilding of the house after the fire, the scars of that episode were still apparent when we moved in for permanent residence, especially downstairs where live embers had eaten into the floors. There also remained a certain amount of primitiveness in addition to the scanty plumbing. Lacking electricity, we also lacked refrigerator, washer, and vacuum cleaner. We shared a telephone with several neighbors on a line festooned from fence post to tree limb, plus an occasional leaning utility pole, along the road from town. And because our water was from a spring that was uncertain in dry weather and under no more pressure than a mild degree of gravity afforded, the only outlets were a half-inch pipe to the kitchen sink and another to the toilet. Being slightly the lower of the two, the toilet took precedence and when it was in use the flow at the sink stopped altogether.

The first time we sought to turn on the water after taking possession of the house we searched for a valve but couldn't find it. So we asked a neighbor.

"It's in the corner of the kitchen," he said.

Since there didn't seem to be anything in the corner of the kitchen except floor, we stopped by his place again and he came along to show us. Sure enough, in a damp little hole under a loose piece of floorboard were the ends of two half-inch lead pipes. Our neighbor pulled a cork out of the pipe that came down from the spring, joined it to the end that led into the house, and bound the two together with friction tape. The water travelled slowly along the pipe that snaked its way up through the floor, over the kitchen door, and along the wall to the sink. As small leaks appeared in the sags where water had collected and frozen, our friend taped them and we began to understand that this was standard local plumbing practice. All of this "water system" was destroyed by the fire, of course, and when we rebuilt we transferred the pipes to the cellar and replaced the cork-and-tape arrangement with a valve and petcock drain. But our pipes have sometimes frozen on a cold night and I have applied the friction-tape procedure often enough. I have even improved on it by closing the split in the pipe with a pair of pliers, then covering it with a well-chewed piece of gum before taping. It's a safer mend, especially if the pipe has been split for some distance, and it lasts for about five years.

As for hot water, our only source was a big copper tea-kettle that always stood on the stove, plus a reservoir built into the side of the stove from which water could be carried by dipper to the dishpan or to the wash basin in the bathroom. Baths as such—if that is what they could be called—were taken in a big galvanized laundry tub set cozily beside the kitchen stove, the main difficulty being that one could get only one part of one's anatomy in the tub at a time.

* * *

So this was home, the heart of Scrivelsby. There was a lot to be done but it was fun to do it. I quickly noted the difference between permanent and temporary residence. When I unpacked, for example, I put empty luggage in the attic with the pleasant feeling that it would stay there. I found permanent resting-places for all sorts of things, from baskets on a rack in the shed to pictures on the walls, candlesticks on the mantelpiece, files in the study, books on the shelves, and, in an old trunk purchased for fifty cents at a farm auction a year or so before, a collection of patchwork pieces for some future quilt—to be made in the course of long winter evenings.

Mark stayed with me for a few days to see that everything was under control, then went on his way, and my mother, who was living in Hanover, came for a visit. She had had six children, of whom I am the eldest, and everyone called her Mom. Even her friends, even the merchant seamen she worked with during the war, even neighbors, called her Mom. Which was odd because she was the least maternalistic woman ever to grace the north country. She offered her six children all the affection and understanding they wanted and suffered agonies when one of us was unhappy or in trouble, but in personal relationships she treated us with a fine detachment, judging us by the same high standards that she applied to herself and everyone else.

Born after her father's untimely death, she was raised by a semi-invalid mother against whom she rebelled as soon as she could. Her natural qualities of courage and independence were further stimulated by a grandmother and a horseman uncle to whom she was devoted. Grown to girlhood, she once confounded an unwelcome suitor proposing to bestow a fraternity pin on her, by saying that of course she'd like to have it;

she collected such pins and wore them as shoe buckles. The next time he called, she did, though in later years I heard her wonder if she'd behaved in just the right way. On another occasion, when the turn-of-the-century equivalent of a wolf waited for her on a bench in Central Park as she rode her horse (under side-saddle, of course), she charged the fellow as he came forward to greet her and remembered looking down on his shoulder as her horse cleared him. Needless to say, that was the last she saw of the wolf. He must have thought her as wild as the wild grey mare she rode. The Banshee, as the mare was called, came from Squadron A of Brooklyn by way of an ardent beau and proved at least as hard to handle as her wild Irish namesake. On this occasion, as on others, she seemed to relish the challenge provided by her rider.

When Dad was courting Mom in the Adirondacks she carried doughnuts in her pockets as they walked along woodland trails, Dad all romance and Mom enjoying the situation hugely. Every time Dad seemed about to propose again (apparently he did it fairly regularly) she offered him a doughnut on the theory that a full mouth makes romance impractical—for the time being, anyhow. In fact, she was engaged three times before finally saying Yes to Dad (appropriately, perhaps, on the eve of Halloween), and I think he always regarded it as a considerable achievement to have secured her heart.

Now, past sixty, she didn't even look matronly, being always too quick and alert and alive to sink gracefully into the rocking chair of advancing age. She had a purposeful walk even when she had no particular purpose in mind. She had a fine sense of humor and a contagious laugh, a keen intellectual curiosity (despite an education that stopped halfway through finishing school), a facility for languages, and a passion for history—qualities that made her delightful to be with and a constant surprise even to her children.

Widowed in her mid-forties, she had made an interesting life for herself compounded of reading, travel, gardening, and living in and fixing up old houses that she bought or rented in a restless sort of way. She kept a weather eye on her children but never lived with the married ones. She would, however, consent now and then to visit one of us who was married, hence the few days she spent with me the spring we declared our independence. What followed changed the course of a year for us and the rest of her life for her.

Mom and I shared a delight in exploring back roads. What lies around this bend, over that rise? A narrow shady wood road with grass growing in the middle of it follows a stream. In a ragged clearing an abandoned farm house tells a story from its sagging porch. We stop and look in through empty windows. A broken dish, an old broom, cracked stained plaster on the walls, and a rusty cook stove on three legs are evidences of desertion. But what a fine big chimney! And there is a glimpse of panelling in the front room. Could the place possibly be restored, we wonder? But of course! We are incurable optimists in the matter of old houses.

A little farther on the road opens out and we see distant meadows that remind us of Switzerland except that there are no snowcaps—nothing above the tree line except sky. At the top of a hill is a sudden long view of the Green Mountains. We crawl the downgrade in second gear, going gently over thank-you-ma'ams, noting small trails that take off here and there and wondering where they go. "Two roads diverged in a yellow wood, and sorry I could not travel both and be one traveler . . ." wrote Robert Frost, and all the enchantment of back roads lies in those words.

So one day during Mom's visit we combined the urge to explore with a quest for a puppy. We put Davis on the back seat of the car for his morning nap (an arrangement of straps kept him from rolling off), and set out to find a litter we'd heard about. The place was on a back road off a back road with three spurs on it, each of which fetched up in someone's yard.

At the end of the first spur we found the puppies all right, but they weren't the kind I wanted. On a knoll at the end of the second spur was a small brick house that made Mom's eyes light up and suddenly I caught the signal: she was in one of those moods when with a little encouragement she'd buy a place she didn't need and probably wouldn't keep very long, but from which she'd get a prodigious pleasure while she had it. For my part I was always ready with encouragement. On inquiry we learned that the house was not for sale, but a place at the end of the third spur was. Mom asked a few questions, discovered that that house had already been restored, and since she liked to do her own restoring we went home to lunch.

That evening a knock at the door denoted the presence of a city person, for a country person in these parts always comes to the back door. I answered the knock. A tall young man stood in the dusk.

"My name is William James," he said. I barely hesitated at the familiar name, and indeed he turned out to be the grandson of the philosopher whose name we know.

"Do come in, Mr. James," I said.

In the living room I introduced him to Mom who was

sitting in a big chair by the fire knitting quietly but with that vibrant quality about her that always made even her quiet moments seem alive. Our guest sat on the couch across from her and there was a pause filled with expectancy. Then he explained his visit. He had heard that Mom was looking for a house; he had one for sale and "didn't want to overlook any bets," as he put it. His was the house we'd heard about that morning, at the end of the third spur of back road.

Mom went into a little act that never fooled anyone who knew her. She made out she wasn't *really* interested in buying a place; just sort of looking around. But as our guest described a white frame house built in 1789, with the original pine panelling, the big stone fireplace and Dutch oven in the living room, I could see by Mom's expression—a kind of clamped-down look designed to hide her excitement—that she was hooked.

We arranged to see the house the following morning. As we approached along a rough little road, up a hill, and then along a spirea hedge in full bloom, I too began to feel that something pretty special was about to happen. A moment later and there was the house, set back of a flagstone terrace in the shade of old sugar maples and butternut trees. It was one of the loveliest old houses we'd ever seen: low in front, with the roof coming down to the front door, white clapboards, green shutters, a big central chimney serving at least three fireplaces, and a long ell out to the back that snuggled up against the rising hillside.

As with our own house, this one was built on a shelf of land, it faced east across a valley, and was backed by pastures and forest. A neglected garden was a challenge to a woman with a green thumb. Across the drive a big gray barn had

32

been converted (evidently at great cost) into a studio, and along a lane was a new barn that was still a barn. The view spread out over the White River valley and surrounding hills. A strip of far highway with cars moving on it and a stretch of railroad following the curve of the river added a distant motion to the scene that emphasized the air of peace surrounding the place. Inside, advance billing as to panelling and fireplaces had not been exaggerated. There were also three bathrooms, insulated outside walls, a furnace, and a hot-water system.

Six weeks later Mom took possession and vowed it was the last place she'd ever own.

"If you keep it," I told her, "I think it will add ten years to your life."

She did keep it but her health had been precarious for some time and she made only six of the ten years I had hoped for. She prophesied she'd die there, and so she did. But before that she gathered us into its orbit (she was good at that) and in a sense made the place ours as well as her own. A lot of living was crammed into those six years and we were part of it—for a while, a very close part of it.

*   *   *

Meanwhile, of course, things were progressing at Scrivelsby. Mom stayed with me for only a week and then returned to Hanover full of her own plans for the future. My husband wound up his affairs at the university, gave and graded his last exams, and then joined us on the farm in time to put in the vegetable garden over Decoration Day weekend. We always plant garden on this holiday because it is about as early as that piece of damp ground can be worked and besides, in this part of Vermont, there is always danger of frost until mid-June.

Planting garden is one of my husband's favorite occupations and he goes at it with a concentration laced with dedication. He takes off his shoes and goes barefoot in the warm, mellow earth, working the plowed and harrowed ground with hoe and rake, lining up his rows, dropping in the seeds, then covering and patting them down with a satisfaction that is almost atavistic. On this occasion the ritual of putting in garden constituted a professor's quick transition from the trammels of the institution to the freedom of the farm.

As we watched each day for the first seedlings to appear (radishes are so satisfactory; they take only a few days to germinate whereas parsley takes weeks), my husband worked up a supply of wood for the stove and fireplaces, cut the grass around the house, scythed the roadsides, and cleared brush from along the stone walls that bound the homestead. (The sight of bare stone walls is another of his passions, one from which he gets an almost visceral satisfaction and I dare not suggest so much as a lilac bush if it threatens to hide a wall). Then he repaired the chicken house and installed a flock of laying hens, fixed up an adjoining pigpen and bought a little pig that he tended with loving care against the day when it would be transferred to the winter larder.

But perhaps the event in those early summer weeks that was to prove the most rewarding in the long run was the purchase of a small German shepherd bitch puppy, for she was to remain an honored member of the family until, as a stiff and rather crotchety old lady of twelve with a bad heart, she had to be put to sleep lest a coronary cause her greater suffering. I had heard of a kennel in a neighboring town and set out to find it. Again, Mom was with me (she loved dogs almost as much as she loved old houses and gardens), and so was my thirteen-year-old stepdaughter, Nan. Nan was staying with us for the summer and loves all young things.

We found the kennels all right. Up a steep dirt road behind a village was a series of chicken coops converted into dog- and living-quarters and presided over by a grey-haired lady in overalls. She quieted the shouting dogs—there seemed to be a great many of them—and we announced our errand.

"I have only one puppy right now," she said. "But it's the best of the litter because I always keep until last the one I'd least mind being stuck with. You can have her if you wish."

She called the puppy out from under a stoop and it was immediately apparent to Nan that we did wish. A gangly little thing, dark brown and buff, the pup was only six weeks old. She came toward us looking a little uncertain as to what was going on but quite willing to find out. Nan gathered her up into her arms and without further discussion we paid our ten dollars and took her home, the journey punctuated by moments of tummy anguish on the pup's part. We named her Dain after the heroine of an English novel that both Nan and I had read with approval.

Figuratively speaking, Dain hung up her hat along with ours thereafter. From the outset she showed an unusual degree of intelligence, even for a dog. She had been with us for only a few days, for example, when she discovered how to open the screen door of the kitchen from the outside by pulling it toward her with her teeth, getting her nose and then her shoulder around it, and wriggling in. One day she tried this with a bone in her mouth, but having to drop the bone to open the door, she found she couldn't retrieve the bone before the door closed, and after several exasperated attempts she finally gave up with an unmistakable look of disgust and flounced into the kitchen without the bone. Later she learned, again on her own initiative, that by opening the door with a paw instead of her teeth she could bring into the house anything she liked.

Dain also adopted Davis, who couldn't talk yet and called her Da; she followed him around and played with him as though he were another pup—which wasn't far from the truth. If he went out after his breakfast while she was still eating hers she would leave her dish and go with him. If I wanted to know where he was I had only to whistle for Dain and both would come running. Once when he woke from his afternoon nap and cried to get up, she left the front of the house where she had been keeping guard under his window, let herself in through the back door, ran upstairs, and scratched at the door of the guest room where my sister-in-law (the only adult in the house at the time) was resting, to arouse her to her responsibilities.

Twice that summer Dain warned me that Davis was heading for the pond by himself. Once, a year or so later, she warned me that he was using an ax: when I failed to get the signal she ran frantically up to the woods where my husband was working and tried to get him to go back with her, but he too failed to get the signal. By that time I had realized something was wrong and went out and found Davis in the barnyard using an ax a good deal bigger than he was and stopped him. Dain returned from the woods while I was there, saw that everything was under control, and quietly resumed her guard.

The only other animal member of the family that summer was a cat that we had had for about three years and who made her home in the barn during our absences from the farm. Granddaughter of a famous local calico called Shirley Temple, Annie was a small, long-haired, bright-eyed ball of tabby fur on the day I brought her home from town in a box. The dog of that day, a collie bitch, indicated her curiosity by a rather close inspection. I held the kitten in my hands and felt her tremble, apparently with fear. But if that is what it was, it was the first and only time she showed fear in all the years she was with us. Indeed, so nonchalant did she become with the dogs that while she was still a kitten she repeatedly allowed a puppy (though not Dain, of course) to maul her in what seemed a really dangerous fashion. Beginning to wonder about her intelligence, we called her by the silliest name we could think of, which was Anniebellie, and in time we shortened it to Annie.

An early bout with distemper kept her small and always a little ragged-looking but seemed to reinforce the toughness of her character. She gained the upper claw over the dogs, made herself boss of them in the house, and taught his manners to each new dog that came on the place. It got to the point where a sharp word from one of us to a dog was the signal for Annie to rush him with claws outstretched, and we've seen her chase Dain ki-yi-ing around the kitchen for some minor misbehavior on Dain's part that had drawn a reproof from us.

But outdoors it was different. There Annie was fair game to the dogs because they could outrun her and she sometimes found it prudent to take refuge in a tree or on a high fence where she could sit in an attitude of balefulness and disgust while the dogs gave voice below. When they had made their point and tired of it they'd go about more interesting business and Annie would leave her perch and come back to the house. Though she was obviously a cat of great character, her judgment always did seem a little in doubt and it was this deficiency that finally led to her suppression a few years later when she had become old, cranky, stubborn, and determined to use the house for purposes that were clearly unsuitable.

*　　*　　*

We proceeded happily through that first permanent summer at Scrivelsby. In August Mom took possession of her house at the end of the road, I fetching her over from Hanover. Though the car was heavily loaded and we were pressed for time, we nevertheless had to stop at the vet's to pick up a puppy that its owners wished to dispose of and Mom couldn't bear to pass up. It was of the long-haired, black-and-tan variety found just about everywhere in the world. Mom named him Abijah, or Byje for short and, mercifully, he turned out to have a strong stomach in a car. At Mom's Place, as it was known to us, a van load of furniture arrived almost as soon as we did. I spent the day helping her get it settled and then brought her back to Scrivelsby for supper.

It wasn't long after that that Mom led up to an invitation to us—not wholly altruistic, as we knew well enough—to spend the coming winter in the barn-turned-studio that stood across the drive from her house. She remarked first on the size of its furnace and the fact that in our house there wasn't any furnace at all. Then she noted the good proportions of the studio, its attractive interior, its enormous fireplace, and its plumbing—again, in a suspiciously off-hand way. To this in our own minds we added certain facts: that although she had a car, she had never learned to drive and had to depend on some member of the family for that chore; that winter storms in Vermont are apt to be severe; that her health was not good; and that if we didn't live close to her she would be alone. Which was unthinkable. Mom was a fiercely independent woman and it must have cost her something to betray her need of help. So we agreed with her rationalizations, accepted her invitation, and planned to move into the studio in September.

Meanwhile there was the winter to prepare for and the manuscript of a new textbook to be started. We took them in order.

CHAPTER 4

Preparing for Winter

BECAUSE OUR RESIDENCE ON THE FARM WAS NOW SET UP ON a permanent basis, it was necessary to think ahead, as farmers do, in the matter of food and creature comfort for the coming winter. Though we didn't make a living off the farm, our income was at least as scanty as that of most farmers so we had plenty of reason to be conserving, frugal, and provident.

Almost everything produced in garden and barnyard can be stored or in some way preserved for the winter larder. Indeed, I can think of lettuce and parsley as the only exceptions. Our vegetable garden did well that summer. Since we now had the promise of electricity in our area in the coming year and there was already electricity at Mom's Place, we bought the biggest freezer we could find—a capacity of twenty-four cubic feet—and installed it temporarily in her pantry. Thereafter it stood as a perpetual challenge to me and I began to freeze early greens—spinach and thinnings from the rows of young broccoli, cabbage, celery, and beets. A neighbor offered me all the rhubarb I could handle (we had only one plant) and I froze eighty packages in two days.

Later came the mature broccoli and cauliflower, baby carrots, and several varieties of beans and corn.

As for fruit, I had long since discovered the healing qualities of an afternoon of privacy gained by the expedient of searching the woods and pastures for wild strawberries, raspberries, black caps, and blackberries, according to the season. After a harassing morning of household chores and response to the needs of a demanding family, a long ramble alone on a warm summer afternoon with a basket on my arm, exploring hidden berrying spots along remote fences, on secluded knolls, and on steep hillsides generally yields two or three quarts of fruit and sooths my spirit into the bargain. But during this first summer in permanent residence I made the most of the availability of wild berries as much for the sake of the freezer as for the moments of privacy that the picking of them afforded me. With the berries, a bushel of peaches (the only purchased item) completed the fruit-and-vegetable section of the freezer—about eight cubic feet.

Next there was the question of meat. Under a modification of our usual contract with the farm operator we now owned part of the herd. So my husband selected a young heifer that didn't seem to promise much as a future milker and, with the help of a neighbor, "skinned her off," as the saying is around here. I shall not soon forget carving that beef in the neighbor's cool dim cellar, nor how good the fresh liver tasted that night and how different from the store-boughten variety.

Our ambition even extended to the purchase of two spring lambs which we tethered in the grass beyond the garden pending weather cool enough for butchering. One of the silly creatures strangled itself on its rope and had to be buried under a shrub where it might still do some good, but its companion was duly stored in the freezer when its time came. Later we added fifty young roosters, several hens that had stopped laying, and fifty pounds of fresh mackerel ordered from the Boston market and shipped in ice the same day as caught. We took the barrel off the train the next morning and by noon the fish were in the freezer. Mackerel is an easy fish to handle because it doesn't have scales. The pig was to join the lot in November when he would have gained an anticipated weight of some 175 pounds. And since November is also the month in which the ten-day legal hunting season occurs, we hopefully left room for venison as well.

In addition to all this frozen food there were the root vegetables—beets, carrots, onions, potatoes, parsnips, and turnips—as well as cabbage, celery, squash, pumpkins, and apples that are preserved merely by storing them in the cellar or, in the case of parsnips, leaving them in the ground until spring, for they become sweeter by freezing. We were not entirely amateurs at this sort of thing but were out of practice and, in any case, still had much to learn.

We did well enough that first season, however, and even better in those that followed. Today my husband chooses an animal with some Holstein or Ayrshire blood in her to offset the leanness of the Jersey, and he can skin her off without help. Where once I carved a beef with a knife in one hand and the book in the other, today I do without the book. I have also discovered that even if the animal presented to me on the pantry table is an old friend, and sometimes it is, once the skin is off it is only a carcass and evokes no qualms. In addition, we have learned to preserve eggs in waterglass in big crocks in the cellar against the season when the laying drops off; to cure bacon and hams and to render down lard;

to put down corned beef and salt pork; to make jams and
jellies, pickles and sauerkraut (this is Nan's specialty); and
even to make soap from the fat that accumulates in home
butchering.

One of the most successful of our food ventures is the
making of great quantities of soup stock from the bones of
a beef carcass. The butchering of a large animal yields a crate
full of bones on which a good deal of meat remains and
there is also the marrow inside them. We saw the bones into
manageable size, crack them with a cleaver, fill two or three
big canning kettles with them, and then stew them for
several hours or leave them on the stove overnight, which,
parenthetically, is yet another advantage of a wood-burning
stove. When the pot cools we clean the meat off the bones,
fill jars with stock and meat, and then can or freeze them.
This procedure yields as much as thirty quarts or more of
fine rich stock from a single animal. The result is best appreciated at lunch on a cold winter day after a morning spent
in the woods or cutting ice on the pond or sweating it out
in the study over a hard chapter.

Perhaps this is also the place to say that under the tutelage
of my mother I learned to make good bread. The family
always knows when this project is afoot, of course, and invariably invents some important reason to be in the kitchen
just as I am about to take the fresh loaves from the oven.
I set them to cool on the counter, with a knife and a dish
of butter beside them. As soon as a loaf is cool enough to
cut, it takes only about half an hour for it to disappear. The
others last a couple of days or so and then I go at it again.
Fortunately I like to make bread and since my brother
operates an old-fashioned stone-burr grist mill, the flour I

use makes a loaf that hardly resembles the soft, neatly packaged article piled on the shelves of the supermarket.

* * *

Our next step was to prepare the studio at Mom's Place for winter residence for ourselves. It made the job easier, I think, that we didn't know what we were getting into.

The studio was a thing to behold. Perched on a side hill overlooking the White River, unprotected from winter gales, its main room was forty feet long, went clear up to the roof-tree, and was lighted by windows in which were four hundred panes of glass, including 144 panes in the great west window that had once been the haybarn door. The views from the studio were such as only Vermont affords, of course, and the architect had apparently been determined that none should be lost for lack of glass through which to see them. An open stairway in the main room led to a wide balcony loft which my husband decided to use as a study. Off the main room was a small bedroom and a big bathroom. Handhewn beams and rafters and timbers were everywhere exposed. The walls were single gray boards outside and painted beaver board inside, with only a sheet of building paper between. Or at least I suppose there was building paper between them; on a cold windy night in the ensuing winter it was easy to believe that the paper had been omitted.

In the basement, which had windows on the lower side, there was a big kitchen and a small tool room that we converted into a bedroom for Nan, for she was to live with us that year and go to school in Bethel. There was also a furnace big enough to heat a hotel (so we were told) but, as it was to prove, not powerful enough to heat the studio. The floor in the basement was hard, cold, damp concrete that would sweat in summer and never warm up in winter. It also had the property, as I was to discover, of making absolutely certain that any breakable object dropped on it would surely break. Nothing bounced, as on a wooden floor some things sometimes do.

But what a place! Native Vermonters, seeing it for the first time, would shake their heads and suddenly become speechless. (Contrary to the Coolidge legend, speechlessness is not a common Vermont characteristic.) The effect was baronial at the very least and we pictured ourselves sitting before a roaring open fire in the big stone fireplace, with Dain and maybe two or three other dogs stretched out on the hearthrug. Since none of the shortcomings of a baronial residence in a Vermont winter impressed themselves on us in August, we went happily forward with our plans and wouldn't have changed them even if we had known what the future held.

My husband's impatience to start his new book soon got the better of his delight in working around the farm and in addition, our financial future depended in part on the royalties that we hopefully anticipated. So I got the loft in the studio ready for him and he took to going down there for several hours each day. Mom offered him his lunch. A favorite meal with him is Irish stew, Mom was expert at making it, and the two of them cemented a new friendship over this delicacy.

Early in September I tackled the main part of the studio. It had never been lived in regularly and took a bit of fixing. As, for instance, the hundreds of panes of glass that I cleaned until my knuckles were raw and I determined that *that* cleaning would have to last a long time. Or the hand-hewn beams that were full of powder-post beetles and had to be

45

painted or sprayed with a poison solution that killed the varmints and nearly got me, too. I hoped that the colonies of spiders that flourished in inaccessible high corners would also succumb to the fumes of the poison but they didn't and we learned to live with them.

By the end of the month everything was in order. We borrowed a truck, my husband took a day off from his writing, and by evening we were settled in our new quarters—pig, chickens, dog, cat, freezer, files, books, and all. The animals were made comfortable in various parts of the barn—the real one, not the remodelled one. Mom in her house across the drive gave us a hearty dinner that night and we understood her silent gratitude.

* * *

Life in the studio soon settled into a routine. We got up at 5:30 on a school morning. While I was busy in the kitchen, Nan dressed Davis and my husband tended furnace and built a fire in the basement fireplace beside which we ate breakfast. Afterward Nan washed the dishes, made her bed and her lunch, and was off to school, catching a ride with a milk truck that called each morning at the adjoining farm and going with it to the main highway where she was picked up by a bus. I saw to Davis' post-breakfast needs, got him ready to go out, called the dogs, and sent them all off together. My husband did barn chores and by 8:30 we were both at work at our desks.

Our system in writing a book—this was the second joint effort on a textbook—is to plan it together, after which my husband writes the first draft. I take it from there to edit for completeness, arrangement, and language. He is the artist,

46

I the craftsman; he gives me a free hand and always has the last word. It is a system that works well with us and has the added advantage of saving time because the second draft follows closely on the first one and is completed about a week later. I had my desk beside an east window in the big room. With my husband in the open loft above we could call to each other when necessary but couldn't see each other, so enjoyed a sense of privacy.

Davis, who was now eighteen months old, was as much a puppy as the rest of the dogs: Dain and Mom's two, Abijah and a border collie called Jehadiah. The dogs seemed aware of their responsibilities as baby-sitters and never left the boy alone. He began to imitate them in funny ways: I once found him trying to dig loose earth with his feet the way they did, and again, pulling the well rope with his teeth because that was what they were doing. If he was in trouble, as sometimes happened, the barking of the dogs gave the alarm. If I missed him I had only to whistle for the dogs to know where he was.

Toward the end of each morning I would stop work in time to get Davis in and prepare lunch, after which he had his nap and my husband and I went back to our typewriters. In the late afternoon he did barn chores again, we sometimes had tea with Mom in her big panelled living room or she came and had it with us, and Nan got back from school. She came part way by bus but then had to walk the mile and a half from the main road carrying not only her books, the mail, *The New York Times*, and her lunch box, but also the gallon can of milk that she had picked up at a neighbor's milkhouse.

After dinner Nan did the dishes and her homework, I read to Davis for a while and then put him to bed, and not too long after that the rest of us turned in. We sometimes thought of the pleasure we had anticipated of sitting up of an evening in front of the fire and savoring the delights of life in a baronial setting, but since the baronial setting didn't include baronial domestic service, the end of the day usually found us well enough satisfied with the work thereof and more than ready for bed.

Meanwhile, after the usual brief cold spell in September, with a night or two of just enough frost to kill the flowers and most of the vegetables, the weather turned to a lovely soft Indian summer that lasted through most of October. Inside the studio the sun shone through the hundreds of panes of glass, the nights were cool enough to require a cozy number of blankets, the mornings were mild and we sometimes had Sunday breakfast sitting in the sun on the little terrace beside the kitchen door. Davis and the dogs were in fine fettle, the pig was putting on weight, we were getting 75 percent production on eggs, and the car wasn't giving any more bother than usual. My mother, independent though she was, seemed to like having us around. The book was progressing well; barring the unforeseen, it looked as though we wouldn't have too much trouble meeting the spring deadline set by the publisher for the completed manuscript.

But some little devil must have been sitting on our shoulders deciding to challenge our ingenuity and our fortitude, because although we did meet the deadline, the unforeseen turned out to be a good deal more familiar to us than the foreseen.

CHAPTER 5

Vermont Winter

OF THE MANY UNFORESEEN FACTORS THAT PUSHED US AROUND that winter, all were directly or indirectly traceable to the weather. It is true that we'd never spent a winter in Vermont before—only the tail end of one—but we knew well enough that they are cold, that the wind blows through unwinter-worthy buildings, and that water freezes in unprotected pipes. But such considerations seemed remote as we went about our work during those fine, soft, hazy Indian summer days.

But the Indians retreated early in November when the weather suddenly turned cold. It had been a dry fall, Mom's spring had fallen alarmingly low, and I had been doing the family wash in cold pond water in a big galvanized tub set on the dam back at our place. By soaking the clothes over-night, next morning they were washable. But when I began to find ice on the tub in the morning I decided the drought might come to an end now and I wouldn't mind.

Except for the discomfort of washing clothes in ice water we didn't object to the dry weather because it prolonged the season of bright autumn foliage for a couple of weeks beyond

49

the usual limit. Indeed, one morning we wakened to find that a gentle but rather heavy wet snow had fallen in the night and accumulated on the still leafy branches of the trees, constituting a considerable burden and bending the branches low. To drive in the car that morning with Mom along a road bordered with maples was to pass through a tunnel of green and red and orange overlaid with the soft white of the snow. By noon the snow was gone but the leaves remained for another two or three weeks until a storm early in November took them off in a single day.

Then the second phase of the fall season set in and we found it as beautiful as the bright one. The frost crept gradually into the ground, making it hard beneath the covering of dead leaves. All of the trees except the evergreens were bare and gray and clearly etched against the sky and the brown hills. The medley of neutral colors and tones—with nevertheless a kind of vitality about them—was poetry in the pastures. Grays and browns of every hue were mixed with patches of copper from the carpet of leaves beneath the beeches, and with the green of pine, spruce, and hemlock. The far hills were a hazy lavender, purple, and blue. On early mornings the higher elevations were sometimes powdered with snow. Then there is the pungent smell of dry leaves as you kick through them on a walk in the woods on a fine crisp day that makes you feel alive. Each year I come alive with the first frost. I love to watch the winter coming on.

In November the pig was transferred to the freezer and so were the roosters. In the week before the ten-day legal hunting season, from the windows of the studio we watched, as we dressed, small herds of deer—eight or ten at a time—moving across the pastures, mingling with the heifers for a moment of friendly grazing, and then disappearing to haunts that only the deer seem to know in this dangerous time of year. As so often happens when the hunting season opened, our hills were full of hunters but not of deer and the freezer space we had saved for venison wasn't used.

Right after hunting season came Thanksgiving, hardly a pause in the routine at the studio for a full-dress family dinner. Thereafter the first few snowfalls were lovely to watch, and as the days grew shorter and colder, the ground stayed white longer until by Christmas it had been white for some time. We assured Davis that Santa Claus would certainly be able to use his sleigh that year, and there was no talk of planes, jets, or satellites.

Davis was of an age to appreciate Christmas for the first time—he was nearly two—and Nan, at thirteen, was still young enough to have a child's eagerness to see what was in her stocking and in the heaps of packages under the tree. The big room at the studio was a perfect setting for Christmas decorations and we had the perfect tree. Two years earlier, my husband had found a well-formed young spruce when he was clearing pasture one day, and had saved it for a future Christmas tree. But a young evergreen can grow very fast indeed and this one was now fourteen feet high. We couldn't have used more than half of it in our own living room but for the studio it was just right. We fetched it down from the pasture along with sacks of ground pine and princess pine and a mass of evergreen boughs. We set the tree against the big west window in the main room in the studio, where it stood silhouetted by day against the light and reflected by night in the many panes of glass behind it.

On Christmas Eve Mom joined us for dinner and afterwards

we decked the tree with lights and trimmed it with her stock of ornaments as well as our own. We made wreaths of ground pine and evergreen branches for the doors, and ropes of ground pine to hang from the crossbeams and the loft. Nan and Davis hung their stockings with due ceremony from the oak mantel and went off to bed. The rest of us arranged a pile of gifts around the tree and then sat by the fire where, warmed by the blaze and hot buttered rum, we stuffed stockings and thought all the sentimental things one thinks on Christmas Eve.

The next morning was one of those miraculous sunrises that occur now and then in a lifetime, but only in the country. The night had been damp and still and cold, and by morning every branch and twig of tree and bush was coated with thick jagged frost crystals. The sunrise was of the flaming red variety that constitutes a warning to fishermen and shepherds in the old saying. For a little while it touched each frost crystal and turned it pink. Everything we could see—hills, pastures, trees, fences—was a frosty, sparkling pink. I had once seen a pink snowstorm, a heavy but limited fall of snow over a valley with the rays of the setting sun shining through it. That was lovely, but this was miraculous, for it transformed everything we could see into a rosy fairyland on a cold clear Christmas Day in the morning.

Children always seem to respond to some private alarm clock set very early on Christmas morning and on this one they could hardly wait for my husband to stoke the furnace and build the open fires before exploring the mysteries of bulging lumpy stockings. After breakfast Mom joined us—she was wearing a red dress and her diamonds and looked like Mrs. Santa Claus from Paris—and we opened the gifts from under the tree. Then Nan and I retired to the kitchen where we spent the rest of the morning, and by the time my brother and his family arrived, the customary copious holiday dinner was ready.

We had improvised a long table in front of the basement fireplace where a fire burned brightly under a mantel decked with candles and evergreens. Mom had loaned me her red damask tablecloth and silver candlesticks, and we set a bowl of pine cones and evergreens as a centerpiece. My heavy white ironstone china completed the table arrangement and looked very Christmassy against the red cloth. From turkey through mince pies we refreshed ourselves with some of my brother's vintage cider and at each stage found the combination to be of gourmet quality.

The morning after Christmas was that day in 1947 when the heavens dumped twenty-six inches of snow on New York City, causing a case of almost total metropolitan paralysis. The edge of the storm also gave us in Vermont a heavy fall but here we know how to handle snow. Men and equipment are out as soon as the snow begins to accumulate on the highways, there is seldom a serious interruption of traffic, and even most of the back roads that are still used in winter (quite a few are not) are quickly cleared. At Mom's Place the town snowplow would toil ponderously up the hill sounding like a locomotive. A great orange monster, it was, with huge wings out in front. If it came at night its powerful headlights announced its approach long before the sound of it came to ear. It would turn around in Mom's dooryard and then lumber off down the hill again like some prehistoric beast, clumsy of movement and small of brain.

*　　*　　*

After that post-Christmas storm the snow kept on coming every day or so and it kept getting colder, too. So by early January we weren't exactly surprised when Mom announced that she guessed, if it was all right with us, that she'd leave her house, her house plants, and her dogs with us and visit another daughter—my pediatrician sister Faith, who had a practice in Connecticut. Faith also had a nice warm apartment and she seldom had trouble with her car.

With us, it was different on both counts. On the day set for Mom's departure, for example, the snow was nearly three feet deep and it was so cold that our car was frozen tight; even the wheels were locked by the frost. So we asked a neighbor to take Mom to the station and they went roaring off down the hill in his battered old pickup, with Mom's heart in her mouth as I well knew, because the optimum comfortable speed for her was thirty-five miles an hour on a good, straight, dry highway. Then we called the garage man to come and get the Olds started.

After that we evolved a car-starting procedure of our own that worked pretty well. We'd take a two-gallon can of hot water to the shed that served as garage, remove the old fur coat that, hopefully, we kept over the radiator, lift the hood, slowly pour the hot water over the manifold and adjacent parts, and then quickly run around, get behind the wheel, and step on the starter. The choke on that car was of the automatic variety, which meant that for the most part it didn't work at all. Nor was it safe to get out and close the hood until the engine was running smoothly. If this system failed, and it sometimes did, then we stayed home, because the margin of success was narrow and when it was exceeded the car seemed to settle down into a morbid kind of crankiness, digging its heels in and resisting all further efforts to start it *that* day. Something to do with a butterfly valve, whatever that is.

After Mom left, the winter came down on us in earnest. One morning when I got up at 5:30 to close the tiny crack of window we allowed ourselves at night, it seemed unusually cold even for that hour. It was still dark, of course, but even so . . . . I looked at the outside thermometer with a flashlight and it registered 24° below zero. When I turned on the tap in the bathroom, no water. No water in the kitchen sink, either. The line had frozen, we supposed, at the point where it went beneath the driveway between Mom's house and the studio, that being the only spot without much snow on it and hence open to the frost. The snowplow had done its job only too well.

On phoning around we learned of a man who specializes in this kind of difficulty and in the afternoon he came with a truckload of equipment. He hitched an electrical wire onto the part of our water pipe that was in Mom's cellar, another to the end that came into the studio, started a generator on his truck, and pretty soon the water was running again. We thanked him, paid him $14, and listened carefully to his caution that thereafter the water would have to be kept constantly running in the kitchen sink because if it stopped it would freeze even quicker than before. Water pipes seem to react that way to artificial thawing, he said.

But during the water shortage of the preceding fall we had trained ourselves to keep all taps tightly closed and it was hard to change this habit. Twice on the following day I rushed to the kitchen to turn the water on after suddenly remembering that I had inadvertently shut it off. But on the third morning when my husband got up to tend furnace, he crawled back into bed again, tucked his head under the covers, and murmured in a small voice,

"The water has stopped."

One of us, we never tried to find out who, had turned the tap off in the kitchen the night before.

After that we didn't bother with running water in the studio any more. We simply turned off the hot water system and set a big galvanized laundry tub on a rack in the corner of the kitchen. Then every morning as part of his regular chores my husband fetched water by the bucketful from Mom's house, filled the tub, and left two full buckets in the bathroom for what scanty washing we allowed ourselves there. For the rest, we used the bathroom in Mom's house. She had left the thermostat of her oil furnace at 55° and although not exactly cozy, her house was warm enough to keep the pipes from freezing. A small electric heater in her bathroom helped in there quite a bit, especially if there was to be the luxury of a bath.

By this time, on school mornings Nan was going down to the main road on skis instead of by the milk truck, which had changed its route and its hours. She carried her books and other gear in a knapsack, left her skis at a neighbor's house beside the highway, picked them up again in the afternoon, collected the gallon can of milk, and toiled back up the hill (no ski tow), always arriving after dark. One morning when she skied down the hill it was so cold she froze the end of her nose. Indeed, the cold was bitter but deceptive too, especially on a bright day. Once when the road was so icy that the car was useless even with chains, my husband walked to the highway in weather that was fine and sunny but 20° below zero and windy. By the time he got there he put his hand on his ear and there was no sensation in it. Then he discovered that both ears were frozen.

On yet another morning the outside thermometer registered 36° below zero, it was 2° below freezing in the kitchen, and there was a sheet of ice on the reservoir tub. Fortunately we didn't have to worry about pipes; they had been useless for some time. I dressed Davis in his snowsuit for breakfast but even so his hands were so cold he couldn't hold his cup of milk. The furnace roared but it was afternoon, when the sun came in the big west window, before the house was anywhere near comfortable. Outside it was beautiful, bright and clear and sparkling, and above all, dry.

On the whole, the cold didn't bother us as much as it might have. For one thing, we dressed for it, with heavy underwear, woolen stockings, and stout boots in addition to woolen outer garments and as many sweaters as needed. I could and often did run across to Mom's house without putting on a jacket. My husband even went to the barn without one if he wasn't going to stay there for long. And cold, moonlit nights Nan took to skiing on the hill behind Mom's house.

It was the dryness that made the difference. One Sunday with the temperature at 30° below zero, for example, it was such a fine clear blue day that we planned to take the family on a wood-cutting expedition to the woods on our own place and have a picnic lunch there. This was something we always enjoyed. We'd build a big fire to keep ourselves and the steel splitting wedges warm—wedges, it seems, crack if they are used at below-freezing temperatures—and then my husband and Nan and I would work on wood while Davis amused himself in various ways. Once he found a big old tree stump from which the middle had rotted out. It was just the size for him to climb into and make believe it was a nest or a playpen or just a stump. For lunch we'd have sandwiches and something to drink that we could heat over the fire. On this day, however, the car was immovably frozen and we stayed home.

Like some evil but intelligent beast with little eyes and a twisted brain, that car always seemed maliciously on the alert to get the better of us and it often succeeded. In addition to being a cranky starter, it was badly balanced and hard to keep headed straight on an icy road. There was a half-mile stretch between the house and a turn at the mailbox on the road to Mom's Place that caused us more grief that winter than any other single difficulty, including the water, because at least we could ignore the frozen water line, and the road we couldn't. A short level stretch at the start of this half-mile gave way, at a right angle that tilted out instead of in, to a long undulating hill at the top of which was home.

In order to make the hill without stopping to put chains on and without changing to second gear (changing on a slick hill was the end of that try), it was necessary to get up a good speed on the level stretch. But not too much speed, because there was that tilted right-angle turn before the climb. If the car failed to make the hill even with the aid of empathetic humping on the part of its passengers, it was necessary to back carefully down and start all over again.

It was in backing that the car showed its fiendish ingenuity, its infallible flair for a ditch. It preferred the kind that is deep and has a high bank against which it could snuggle in the snow in a drunken, lopsided way, looking sodden and stubborn and it's-all-your-faultish. To get the monster out was an engineering proposition that entailed fastening the chains on both rear wheels while one of them was deep in snow, this without moving the car. It is a special technique and we became pretty good at it.

It would have been much easier, of course, to put the chains on before trying the hill at all, and this any prudent person would have done. But the chains were messy enough to put on under the best of circumstances. We always came up wet on the knees from having knelt on the road, and wet on the arms from having embraced the wheel in an effort to hitch the inside catch. Also, chains were not often needed except on that short half-mile and there was always a sporting chance that we might make it on the first try, or maybe on the second, or even on the third. There was a nice element of gamble here and the possibility of success was often just enough to tempt us. Especially my husband, who is an incurable optimist about mechanical things.

One night when he had been to a meeting in town I saw the headlights of the car as he returned along the road from the highway, saw them make the turn at the mailbox, gather speed, and then—nothing. I listened for the sound of the car coming up the hill, but there wasn't any. I was already undressed for bed and had been reading before the fire, but I knew that putting on chains at night with half the car in the ditch was a two-man job; someone had to hold the light. So I dressed, took an extra flashlight, and set off down the hill to lend a hand. Sure enough, it was needed. It took more than a hour that time and we got back cold and wet from having to dig a wheel out from the snowbank before putting the chain on it. A hot nightcap of the liquid variety helped quite a bit.

*   *   *

59

By contrast, Davis was about as little trouble that winter as any two-year-old could be. Partly, I suppose, it was because he spent so much of his time outdoors under the dogs' supervision instead of mine. He couldn't talk beyond a few words yet, but made as much noise as though he could, and he understood nearly everything said to or about him.

He knew, for example, that he was not to interrupt his Dad at his writing in the loft, and that the staircase there was forbidden territory except when he was asked to announce that lunch was ready, and he made the most of that opportunity. In the kitchen when I was about to serve it up, I'd give the signal, and Davis, who'd been waiting for it, would tear off up the stairs on all fours for safety and more noise (he could slap the steps with his hands as well as pound them with his feet), yelling and shouting as he went, to run across the big room and clatter up the stairs to the loft in a way that conveyed the message beyond any doubt.

Like the elephant's child, Davis also had an insatiable curiosity. In addition, he loves salt, and one day when he was exploring in the back of a closet off the big room he found a bag of rock salt we kept there to sprinkle on icy steps and walks. He must have eaten quite a lot of it before he began to feel the effects. Coming out of the closet, he stood amazed for a moment while I watched inquiringly from my desk, then opened his mouth and without apparent effort or distress, lost his breakfast.

The effect of eating some of his Dad's pipe tobacco, however, was more lasting. At lunch one day he seemed out of sorts and without appetite, so I sent him upstairs to wait until we had finished. When I went up to get him ready for his nap I found him sitting quietly in a big chair with his head against the back of it and looking pretty green. I could see no reason for his distress, however, so I put him to bed. A little later, unmistakable sounds from the bedroom caused me to investigate in a hurry, and it was immediately apparent that pipe tobacco was involved. Fortunately he got rid of it after a few more tries. By four o'clock he seemed quite restored and a little pleased with himself as he sat on the couch before the fire with the rest of the family waiting on him.

An interesting clue to a small boy's character was provided one day by his reaction to the high snow banks which by now lined the sides of the drive between Mom's house and the studio. By the passage of the snowplow every day or so, these banks had been pushed up to a height of six feet or more; they were so high that standing in the drive we couldn't see over the top of them.

One morning after I had let Davis out with the dogs, I heard him yelling and crying, and going to the window, saw him trying to climb one of these snow mountains. The surface was hard and icy, his boots were smooth, and the more he tried and slipped back, the more angry and determined he grew and the more slippery the track became. Again and again he started up the bank, clutching for handholds, tears streaming down his cheeks, and uttering his angriest protest of WEE! WEE! WEE! Finally he moved a little to the side, got a foothold, and crawled to the top. But he was too angry and exhausted to enjoy his victory. He just sat there for a while and cried, then got wearily down and came to the door where I gathered him in and comforted him.

One afternoon he followed the dogs to the top of a high retaining wall behind the studio and when they jumped down and then back again, he could only jump down. He cried, the dogs barked—Dain in that special tone I had learned to recognize as a shout to "Come and see to the boy!" I heard them above the clatter of the typewriter and went to the rescue. This time he didn't need comforting but went happily off again with the dogs.

In addition to the unusual amount of snow and cold that winter—the cold was so persistent that we had thirty inches of ice on the pond where generally we had only about half that amount—there was also a recurring wind that piled great drifts of snow around the houses and sometimes across the roads where they were not protected by snow fences. In the studio we were usually too busy to notice the wind very much during the day. But at night when we sat before the fire for a few moments before going to bed, the sound of the creaking rafters as they seemed to try to join the gale in its wild course over the Vermont hills impressed itself on our attention. The whole studio shook and creaked and from time to time a fresh breeze came down from the region of the rooftree. I have always thought that the sound of "the wind in the willows" must be a very lovely and soothing thing, connoting all sorts of dreamy idling along pastures and riverbanks on a summer day. By contrast, the sound of the wind in the rafters is a great blustery thing, connoting turbulence and distress on a winter night. Once, before Mom went to Connecticut and she was spending the evening with us, the sound of the swaying rafters was so alarming that she went back to her own house, frankly admitting that she felt unsafe in the studio on such a night. To us, the sound became routine and the breeze from the region of the rooftree was countered by plenty of warm clothing and a roaring fire on the hearth. Old buildings that are pegged together instead of nailed are tough.

They may rot and fall to pieces but they seldom come apart by force that is not deliberately planned and executed.

*   *   *

There were several events of that winter that might be taken as marking the high spot of adventure for us. There was, for example, the night on which the local Rotary Club received its charter, early in February. Because of lack of space, the only way the ladies could be included in the ceremony was for them to wait on table, which we did. But it was 20° below zero outside, and to wear store clothes, including nylons that seem to act as conductor between frost and skin, and to stand around after the celebration while frozen cars were unfrozen by a devoted Rotary brother who operated a local service station, was an experience that I'd not care to repeat. The steaming cars were finally thawed and started, but it was after midnight before we got home. There we found that the furnace had burned itself out and we had to get it going again before turning in.

Then there was the time I drove to meet my husband on the early morning train from New York and the radiator of the car froze on the way to town. Great clouds of steam began coming from it but there was no sense in stopping on the highway at five o'clock in pitch dark and no help anywhere. I eased fearfully into town but of course no service station was open. A pleasant young man at the station who was also waiting for the train advised me to leave the engine running at idling speed under a blanket. This procedure succeeded in thawing the radiator, all right, but by that time all the antifreeze had boiled away. If I added water it would quickly freeze again unless I left the engine running.

At that point it turned out that the train was to be more than an hour late. I had left Davis asleep in his crib and knew he would soon be waking and needing attention right away. But I could not reach Nan by phone in her basement room—the only phone was in Mom's house. I began to feel the pressure from both sides and the middle, so to speak, and finally left a message at the station for my husband to find some other means of transportation, filled the radiator with water, tucked a blanket around it, and started driving back to the studio.

Not content with freezing its insides, however, the Olds now developed an ominous-sounding cough on the hills and I wondered if I'd have to walk the last part of the way, but I didn't have to. Back at the studio, I tried to drain the radiator but found that the knob of the petcock in the block was missing. I tried pliers but succeeded only in freezing my hands. Finally I gave the whole thing up and left the engine running under its blanket, hoping there was enough gas to keep it going until my husband arrived and took over, which in due time he did. After breakfast we drove back to town, got a new petcock and another gallon or so of antifreeze, and applied the mechanical equivalent of soothing syrup to the ominous-sounding cough.

Perhaps the highest adventure of all during that winter was Davis' second birthday, early in February. My husband had gone to Washington to attend a conference, it was Sunday, and Nan and I had planned to take Davis and visit my brother and his family on their farm some thirty miles to the south. The day dawned with uncertain weather, however, and standing at an east window at the studio and watching a sudden heavy snow coming down, we wondered: should we or shouldn't we risk it? We decided to give it a try.

Once on the road, we found it slippery under the new snow, and the Olds, faithful to its perverse nature, promptly slid into a ditch. Nan got out to push, a procedure at which she had become competent, while I did what I could at the wheel. The bottom of Nan's parka caught on the rear bumper and as the car cleared the ditch she was dragged on her tummy for several feet. She got back in the car a little shaken but not badly hurt. Pretty soon the snow stopped and without further incident we arrived at my brother's place.

We had a fine birthday dinner in his big kitchen and a beautiful cake with three candles on it, two for years and one to grow on. Davis opened his presents and seemed pleased. In mid-afternoon we packed up and started home, reaching our own back road about an hour before dark. Although the snow had been brief it had been heavy and was followed by a sharp wind that cleared stretches of road in some places and piled drifts in others. I engaged the Olds on the first hill at a good speed and, rounding a bend at the top, slammed into a drift that was higher than the car. But it was close to a neighbor's house and with the aid of shovels that we always carried, and his tractor (he had to hitch onto the front end of the Olds and lift it, wrecker fashion), we got free. By dint of rushing succeeding drifts, which were smaller, we smashed through until, rounding the turn at the mailbox, a big one stopped us. The Olds plunged into it headfirst and when we came to rest, its rear wheels were off the ground.

Nan went off to another neighbor's in search of another tractor while I set to work with a shovel and Davis sat on the front seat and waited expectantly for what might happen next. It was getting dark now and much colder. Even my heels were cold and, as Nan remarked when she came back, when your heels are cold you've really had it. The neighbor wasn't home so there was no tractor and nothing for it but to leave the car and walk the rest of the way. The car was loaded with a box of apples, jugs of cider, the remains of the cake, and other items contributed by my brother, all of which would doubtless freeze if we abandoned them. They would have to be toted and so would Davis.

Nan took what she could and went ahead. I laid a rug on the snow, placed Davis in the middle of it, hitched the four corners together, slung him on my back, and set out. He was so quiet that after a while I worried lest he was smothering, but a question from me brought a grunt from him and I was reassured. I met Nan coming back down the hill on her skis. She made three trips on them before all our gear was back at the studio. The furnace had behaved well during our absence and the place was warm. We had a good hot supper. Davis threw his birthday crayons to the dogs who found them tasty. We finally went to bed, feeling rather pleased with ourselves and none the worse for the exertions of the day.

The following morning was its usual bright sunny cold self and my husband was due on the early train. I phoned a message to the station saying I couldn't meet him. He got a ride as far as the first big snowdrift and walked from there. From a window in the big room I watched him as he strode along the lower road at a good clip, carrying bag and brief-case. I had a fine breakfast waiting for him: sausage and eggs and coffee and a mountain of hot bread. Later the snowplow rescued the car—had to, in fact, in order to complete its appointed rounds. But it took a lot of dragging and pushing—about half-a-mile's worth—before the wheels of the car unlocked and the engine consented to turn over. A dent in the metal fanny of the Olds was to be a lasting reminder of the incident.

*   *   *

Such was our winter in the studio. On the plus side—and most of it was—the little devil who would have delayed our writing succeeded merely in testing our mettle. Whatever the difficulties of wind and weather, of frozen car and frozen water pipes, with which we had to cope, the writing was never held up for long. The deadline was approaching and it didn't scare us. Also on the plus side was the fact that the combination of cold weather and not too sharp a difference in temperature between the inside of the studio and its surrounding windy hillside, built up our resistance and made us feel wonderfully well. Even the catastrophes and inconveniences precipitated by our guardian devil constituted a kind of challenge and were sort of interesting, even if we didn't care to encounter them again right away.

Above all, I think, we had enjoyed that sense of peace you find in Vermont, especially in winter. You seem to get so much more done—and effortlessly, too—simply because you're not battered about as you are in the city. When it's quiet, you seem somehow to be connected and all in one piece; you can think, and savor the good simple things in your life that are easily overlooked when you are bounded by the formality of the institution and beset by the disintegrating forces that erode the usual urban existence.

We chose a cold grey morning on one of the stormiest days of February to make the final decision, whether to continue our experiment in freedom or take advantage of the year's leave of absence from the university and return to the shelter of the regular monthly pay check. It was no trouble at all to decide to stay free.

CHAPTER 6

Vermont Spring

THE BREAKUP OF WINTER ANNOUNCED ITSELF THAT YEAR WITH water—lots of it. If excessive cold was the dominant theme of winter in the studio—and I do mean *in* it—then water was the theme of spring.

It was March now, and sugar season. We were still deep in snow and nights were freezing. But days were sunny and mild, causing the sap to rise in the maples for any who would tap them, hang buckets, gather the sap, and boil it down to the proper consistency. It is a wonderful time of year. The taste of maple sap right from the bucket is different from anything else in the world. A sugar house sits in a cloud of steam generated from the sap boiling in a big flat pan that is four feet wide and anything up to twelve feet long; and again, the smell of the sap is special and indescribable. A picnic lunch in the sugar house always includes eggs hard-cooked in the boiling sap.

At the beginning of sugar season a heavy wet snow lies everywhere, but it goes off fast and by the end of sugaring, marked by buds on the maples and the sound of peepers in the ponds, most of the snow is gone.

One night in the studio during this season, when all the household was asleep, Nan in her basement room was wakened by water dripping on her face. She got up, sleepily moved her cot out of the line of drip and went back to bed. A little later she was wakened again. This time she realized that something was wrong and went upstairs to investigate. The whole back end of the big room was afloat. Following the mild days, a mild night was melting the snow on the sloping rear of the roof and water was coming in under the setback of the eaves. From there it dripped down through the top of the window frames, splashed onto window sills, bookcases, my work table, the manuscript, and the floor, where it spread out and dripped down through the cracks into Nan's room below.

Without waking her father or me, though all this was taking place right outside our bedroom door, Nan rescued the manuscript and working papers from my desk and piled them on the stairs to the loft, this being the only safe high ground. Then she mopped up what water she could, set pans under the worst of the drips, went back to bed with a raincoat over her face and went to sleep again. Thanks to her resourcefulness there was no major damage to the manuscript, which in time dried out pretty well. But as the drip seemed likely to recur, we moved Nan out of her little cellar room and over to a spare room in Mom's house.

The deadline set by the publishers for the completion of the manuscript was the end of March and we were right on schedule despite the flood and other interruptions. Chapters in first draft came down to me from the loft at more or less regular intervals and two or three days later each had been reworked, retyped, and added to the pile of completed work on my desk. When the last of the chapters was finished, the boss took them all back to his loft and reread them, making final changes and corrections. Then a few days before the deadline I wrapped the whole thing in a big package and we sent it off to New York.

In our experience, sending off the completed manuscript to the publisher is the high point of all the work that goes into the making of a book. As we write, the work gathers momentum, and when it stops and the manuscript has been sent off there is a release of tension accompanied by a strong feeling of achievement. A little like the cackling of a hen after she's sat on a nest for some time and finally managed to produce an egg. By contrast, the first sight of the book between hard covers several months later is a bit of a letdown.

"Well," you think, as you handle it for the first time, "so that's what it looks like." (I don't think a hen ever goes back to look at her egg.)

Then you open it and read a little here and there and it seems better than you remembered. But the sense of elation is gone. The reason, I suppose, is that the time between the completion of the manuscript and the publication of the book is largely occupied with messy jobs like making changes and corrections suggested by publishers' readers, approving or disapproving changes made by publishers' house editors (if you disapprove it may mean an argument), then carefully reading galley and page proof, and at last making an index at top speed so as not to delay the printer. None of this is very interesting and the satisfaction of finishing it doesn't compare with the satisfaction of having said your say as well as you can. The sense of achievement is correspondingly less.

*   *   *

As soon as we had sent the manuscript off, my husband and I turned to the next family project, which was to build a new woodshed onto our own house. The existing one was large enough for summer residence with only a cookstove and a fireplace as consumers of wood. For year-round purposes we figured we'd need something like sixteen cords of wood, and a cord is four by four by eight feet. We also wanted a place to park the car out of the weather if not out of the cold. And in addition, since we had the promise of electric power, we needed a pantry to accommodate the freezer, which was to be moved up from Mom's house. We seemed to be gathering quite a few needs that we'd never had before.

To satisfy this particular set of needs, we arranged on a day when the snow was still deep on the ground to meet at our place with a carpenter neighbor to lay out the new shed. I waded into the middle of the vegetable garden hip deep in snow to get a good view of the south side of the house. My husband held one end of the measuring tape against the existing shed wall, the neighbor took the other end and started walking, and when he had gone about as far as seemed right I stopped him. He made a note of the distance on the tape, we rounded it out to an even number of feet, and he drove a stake through the snow to mark the spot. Then we decided the height on the side of the house to which the shed rooftree should reach, and talked about arches on the front, an attic, and materials. A few days later the neighbor set to work and my husband joined him as assistant.

One day when my husband was thus occupied, I spent the morning working on files in the big room at the studio, and when I stopped to go get lunch, as I went down the stairs to the kitchen, I saw a large puddle before the fireplace.

"My goodness," I thought, "that's an awfully big puddle for a dog to make!"

Then I remembered that the dogs were outside with Davis, and when I investigated I found that water was seeping in under the partition separating the kitchen from the coal bin.

I mopped up the water, started lunch, called Davis and the dogs in from their play, and then noticed that the puddle was there again and bigger than before. This time when I mopped, the water kept on coming. Somewhere in the wall behind the coal bin was a lusty leak. In later years a man with a dowsing stick discovered a subterranean stream flowing under that part of the studio, but I didn't know that when I saw this first evidence of its springtime vigor.

I mopped again, quickly got Davis his lunch, mopped, urged Davis on, mopped, rushed him upstairs for his nap, ran back to the kitchen and mopped some more. Now the water was coming in faster than I could take it up and I began to feel like the sorcerer's apprentice. Not knowing the magic word any better than he did, I ran out to the barn for the wheelbarrow, loaded it with all our kitchen gear, removed the fuse to the electric stove and the refrigerator, then abandoned the whole mess and went back to my desk.

By the time my husband returned at the end of the afternoon the kitchen was flooded, the high doorsill between the kitchen and the terrace acting as a kind of dam. Before taking off his boots my husband transferred the wheelbarrow to Mom's kitchen and for the next two weeks we cooked and ate over there.

After a day or so when no more water seemed to be coming in the studio kitchen, I got rid of what was on the floor by shovelling it out the door with a big square scoop shovel, but after everything was all nice and dry another flood occurred. By this time the experience was old stuff and I merely went to work with the shovel again—my husband was still carpenter's assistant up at our place—and when all danger of another incident seemed past we moved our kitchen gear back to the studio.

Water also plagued us in yet another way that spring, for as the snow went off, the mud came on. Mud occurs, it seems, not only when earth and water come together in a rain or in the mud pies we make as kids, but even more when the frost has got deep into the ground during the winter and gradually comes out under the benign influence of the warm spring sunshine. This kind of mud is common on back country roads that are badly drained, that have not been gravelled, and where clearing by the snowplow permits the frost to go very deep. A depth of four or five feet is pretty normal most winters, but it may be as much as seven or eight feet if the winter has been a severe one, and this one had.

In the north country, mud season is philosophically accepted and practically coped with, except by city folk who seem to be terrified of it. The onset of mud is carefully watched. Stores of food and grain for man and beast are laid in and a so-called mud vacation is arranged for the schools. For a while, beginning generally sometime in March, warm days make the roads slippery and rutty but they freeze solid again at night and it is possible to get through early in the morning, and even back again if one is quick. The mailman who travels miles of back roads is a good source of information as to how things are going.

"They're soft," he may tell you, "but they haven't broken through yet." When they do, he leaves the mail at the box

74

of the neighbor the nearest to you that he can reach, and you fetch it from there.

As traffic and the season progress, the ruts become deeper, softer, and more wavering. You try to avoid them and succeed merely in making new ones. You lurch from one to another that seems—but generally only seems—not quite so bad. Sometimes you don't quite make it and the hind wheels of the car continue in the original ruts while the front wheels go along in a different set, in which case the car labors forward like a dislocated crab. Sometimes if they're deep enough you can't get out of the first set of ruts at all. To find yourself in this kind of impasse and headed for an especially mushy spot that has broken through so that it's part bread dough and part jelly to a depth that buries the hub caps, is to experience a sense of inevitable disaster that is nearly always justified. Once stopped in this kind of dough one can sometimes place a flat stone and then a jack under an axle, raise the wheels enough to put more stones under them as paving and in front of them, and then with much toil and trouble and calling on the Lord, get out of that particular spot. Almost always the help of a tractor, preferably a crawler, is the better part of valor and much easier on the Lord.

Before the days of the jeep—and for us this was before— a road in this condition was impassable by car for anywhere up to two or three weeks. Either you left the car at home or at the home of a neighbor who lived near the blacktop, and in between you used a horse if you had one, or you walked. The best solution was to stay home.

On behalf of Vermont back country it is only fair to say that when dirt roads are properly ditched and gravelled, as increasingly they are, and you own a jeep, as increasingly you do, the trials of mud season are much less than formerly. However, I can find it in my heart to regret this. There is a wonderfully pleasant feeling about knowing that you can't get off the place, and, more important, no one else can get to it. It is almost like being snowbound, provided that in each case, of course, you have plenty of food and fuel on hand. There isn't much to do except keep the fires going and then settle down in a comfortable chair, put your feet up, and read. It is only the restless desire to go places that causes trouble.

As for us during that spring at the studio, we had thought that since the road to Mom's Place was hilly it would be well drained, but it turned out that there were springs lurking under parts of it and we needed no dowser to find them for us; they were evident on their own showing. Going down the hill one morning the Olds sank into one of these soft spots until its nose was nearly buried and it looked like a huge dog digging for a bone. In disgust we left the thing there for a couple of days before jacking it out. After that it stayed in the garage and we settled down to enjoy our privacy.

*   *   *

Yet another sign of spring was the dehibernation of skunks and porcupines as these little animals began to come out of their winter quarters and move about in the woods again. This would not have bothered us had we not had three dogs and all of them young enough to be aggressively inquisitive about such animals. Older dogs know enough to keep out of the way but young ones, especially in a group, behave like a bunch of small boys.

Vermont Spring

We first became aware of the skunks when the dogs began
to come in smelling of the fact that their curiosity had got the
better of their good sense. The climax occurred one night
when they had got a worse dose than usual and it was clear that
the studio wasn't big enough for them and for us too. We
couldn't let them stay outside because they'd fuss to get in
and everyone knows the effect of a barking dog on human
sleep. So my husband took them over to Mom's house and shut
them in a small vestibule. The snow had not yet all gone off
from around the house, however, and the day had been mild
but the night was freezing, and the result was a solid sheet of
ice on lawns and driveway. My husband had gone out in his
bedroom slippers, and returning from his mission he lost his
footing and crashed onto the icy drive. The fall gave him a
concussion that kept him in bed for two days. Fortunately,
by that time the dogs seemed to have largely satisfied their
curiosity about skunks.

But not so with porcupines. We were dining one evening
with friends in Bethel when Nan phoned that the dogs had
come in with quills in their faces, and Dain had a lot of them.
Our host instructed us as to the proper procedure in such
cases, loaned us a pair of pliers (some types are unsuitable),
and we drove back to the studio where we found Nan trying
to comfort the three young idiots. One by one we held them
to the floor and pulled out the quills. A quill is only about an
inch long but it is tough, it contains an irritant poison on the
end of it, it is barbed in such a way that to pull it out brings
flesh along with it, and a dog's nose is a tender organ. We
found that three people to one dog are not too many when
the dog is big, as all of these were, and transformed by pain
into a squirming mass of muscle. Dain was more cooperative

than her colleagues, seeming to sense that the operation was a necessary one and that we were trying to help her.

When the operation was over, all three dogs acted a little crestfallen and foolish and retired to their various favorite spots in the big room to lick their noses and ponder the ways of porcupines. We hoped that the experience would be a final one, and for Mom's two it was. But Dain was above all such cause-and-effect nonsense. When she saw a porky she had to make *sure* that she couldn't handle it. On one occasion I think she must actually have killed one because she came back to the house with hundreds of quills sticking out all over her face. They were in her ears, her eyelids, her lips, nose, mouth, gums, between her teeth, in the roof of her mouth, and back down into her throat. That time we took her to the vet and he anesthetized her. How her eyes escaped I can't imagine.

Even after that experience Dain continued to worry porcupines and we developed a standard technique for dealing with the situation. In the barn we found an old two-tined pitchfork. When Dain needed dequilling we put her head between the tines and pushed them down into the soft earth of the woodshed floor. Then by sitting on her body, one person alone could do the job of extraction. Even Dain seemed to prefer this method. Under the gentler procedure she felt obliged to exert some degree of self-control but with the pitchfork method she was free to make as much fuss as she liked and it didn't delay the operation.

In time she became very blasé about the whole business. One day after we had returned to our own place and I was typing in the upstairs study, I noticed her trotting down the road toward the house. A few moments later she let herself in at the kitchen door, came upstairs, and brought herself

78

to my attention by sticking her bristly nose into my bare leg (I was wearing shorts). Then she looked at me as though to say,

"Come, let's get on with it."

She led the way down to the shed, I applied the pitchfork and pliers, she squirmed and fussed, and when I had done she trotted off again about her business (which I hoped wasn't another porky) and I went back to mine.

During all this early spring season in the studio we were still without legitimate running water indoors. March passed and part of April and still no water where it belonged, though of course there was plenty elsewhere. The frost must have gone very deep indeed. The last of the snow disappeared leaving the countryside bare and wet and soggy and sort of dirty. For me, two or three weeks at this time constitute the only ugly season of the year, before much green has begun to show and repair the damage of the winter. But despite this soggy sign of spring, our taps still ran dry, as the saying is—an odd sort of phrase, when you come to think about it.

The frost finally gave way at five o'clock in the morning on April 14. While I was still in a semiconscious state between sleep and waking I heard a thin clear sound of trickling water that quickly grew stronger. It was water coming into the toilet tank in the adjoining bathroom for the first time since early January and no sound could have been sweeter. I got up quickly, turned on the taps in the basin, and water came forth. It was the same in the kitchen—a fine strong flow of fresh water at the sink. I think it was this day more than any other that finally divided spring from winter for us that year.

A barber in a neighboring town was cutting my husband's hair one day and talking about the hard Vermont winters.

He was pushing eighty, he said, and his family had been after him for some time to go south during the cold weather. Many Vermonters do, not as vacationers but to work at some job that takes them away from their native state for a time when the sun is bright but the temperature low.

"All the same," commented the barber, "I never could bring myself to leave here because when spring comes it happens on a certain particular day, and it's one I wouldn't miss."

He was right. On a certain day that may occur any time between the end of March and the middle of May, spring suddenly arrives. It may turn cold again and there may even be snow, but the day itself is unmistakable. Once in our experience it occurred on April 1. Snow was still deep on the ground but the day was so warm and lovely that for the first time since the onset of winter I opened doors and windows and let the breezes waft through the house.

More dramatic was a certain May 10. Spring had been coming on very slowly and by the morning of that day the trees everywhere were in their early tender green stage of leaf just beginning to unfold. As we looked out the kitchen window at breakfast toward the pasture, the hazy tender quality of young leaves was like a shaded pastel mist on the land. The day turned out bright and beautiful and much warmer than any we'd had. I dug dandelion greens for lunch and we drank a glass of sherry on the lawn. By the end of the afternoon, we suddenly realized that all of the misty colors among the trees had gone and in their place was the definite green of fully opened leaves. All of this in the course of a few hours and we might have seen it actually happen had we been looking for it. The next day the weather turned cloudy and cold again. Sometimes there will even be a snowstorm after the leaves are fully out; I recall one that occurred in the third week of May, and I believe it's a matter of record in Vermont that snow has fallen in every month of the year. Perhaps that's why the Vermont climate is said to consist of nine months of winter and three months of hard sledding.

*   *   *

We couldn't leave the studio that spring to return to our own place until Mom came back to her house, and she couldn't do that until the roads hardened enough to make it possible to get a car in from the highway. We were still at Mom's Place, therefore, when in the middle of April a shipment of several thousand young pines was delivered to our own place and they had to be planted right away.

My husband has a regard for trees that amounts to a passion. He plants them, watches over them, and tends them with loving devotion. To find one that has been hurt causes him a pain that is almost visceral. In addition to their beauty, however, he is keenly aware of their usefulness in a soil-conservation program and of their economic worth at various stages of maturity. (Though I have yet to see him cut one for an economic purpose.)

I first became aware of this passion soon after we bought our place, for each time that we spent so much as a few days there, he'd be out with a pick and shovel and wheelbarrow, digging up young maples, birches, oaks, and evergreens and transplanting them around the homestead. We had had the place for four years when we joined the district program of the federal Soil Conservation Service and planted our first batch of commercial trees—several thousand pine seedlings set out on the slope above the south pasture and visible from our kitchen window. Now nearly twenty years later those trees are more than thirty feet high as they stand massed against the skyline.

Every spring since the first planting, the setting out of young pines on land too rough for pasture takes precedence over everything else on the farm. When the seedlings are delivered, all available help in the neighborhood is rounded up, and for a day or so, men and boys and sometimes girls are tramping over the rocky upland in pairs, one with a mattock and the other with a bucket of seedlings in a little water to keep the roots moist. The man with the mattock clears a small space of undergrowth, makes an incision with his instrument, takes two paces and does it again. The man with the bucket tucks a seedling into the incision, tamps the earth around it with his foot, and goes on to the next incision. By this means thousands of trees may be planted in a single day. Not all of them live, of course, but gaps are filled in as they appear in later years.

In eighteen years we've planted around 150,000 pines on something like one hundred acres of submarginal land. When it comes time to weed them out for pulp it will be money in the bank, and when they become timber it will be a lot more, for our children if not for us. And in the meantime the satisfaction afforded my husband by the operation is something that has become as necessary to him as his daily bread. Of all his priorities, including me, I think his trees come first!

After planting the trees that spring, we marked time for a while pending Mom's return from Connecticut. The weather was mild, the maples were in bud, and there were the beginnings of new grass in the fields and meadows. A neighbor turned his registered Jersey heifers into a pasture above the studio and Dain took advantage of their youthful inexperience to exercise her sense of fun, combined with some ancient instinct to hunt, at their expense and nearly at ours as well. She would go up to the pasture, select a likely-looking heifer, and run around her in a circle, nipping at her nose and her heels as often as possible. Dogs will hunt smaller game that way, especially woodchucks. When the victim is exhausted and dizzy from turning to face the circling dog, the dog senses it and dashes in for the kill. Fortunately, we discovered Dain's little game in time to prevent the kill, which would have cost us something like $150 a head.

To cure Dain and save the family exchequer, my husband put her on a leash and took her back to the pasture among the heifers. Then he broke a stick from a wild apple tree and gave her a sound beating while the heifers stood in a circle and watched with the natural curiosity of their kind. Never one to hide her feelings, Dain yelled her anguish. She also apparently decided that this was serious, refrained from exercising her usual stubbornness, and thereafter left the heifers alone.

Mom finally returned at the end of April bringing with her another puppy, this time a black Labrador whom she named Gideon. That gave her three dogs, which was the way she liked it. A few days later we packed our belongings, loaded them on a truck, and went home.

Among the things we took with us was a big basket containing Annie and four kittens that she had presented to us just a few days earlier. When it was clear that her confinement was approaching along with the date of our departure, I had tried to prevent her from giving birth in the barn or some other inaccessible place by suggesting to her various locations in the studio where I thought she might be comfortable and safe from the dogs. She seemed to give due consideration to my recommendations but also had some ideas of her own. One was a carton of government reports in my husband's loft. After tearing some of them up to make a nest, she changed her mind and looked for something better. She even explored behind a big picture leaning against the wall over the wide stone mantelpiece in the big room. It wasn't hooked to the wall and she knocked it down onto the stone hearth where it shattered and nearly frightened her into a premature confinement right there. I offered her a box with clean rags in it under the stair, and also a basket on a high workbench in Nan's room, but so far as I could see she wasn't ready to commit herself.

Then one evening as we returned from a visit with friends, Annie met us at the front door and seemed excited. She rubbed herself against my legs and made mewing sounds, then headed for the stairs to the kitchen, stopping to see if I'd got the idea and was following. Thinking she might be hungry I did follow, but she went right on through the kitchen and jumped into the basket in Nan's room, then purred and rubbed against my hands, looking very pleased with herself and saying as clearly as anything that her time had come. Sure enough, the next morning there were four kittens in the basket and Annie looking as proud and happy as any new mother. To show them to me she lay down and nursed them, and I admired them and praised her and told her she was a real good girl.

When we returned to the farm I asked Nan to put the basket of kittens in the barn in a place that would be safe from dogs, and this she did. But the following morning when

I opened the kitchen door to the woodshed, there was Annie, looking distressed. She ran past me through the kitchen and the hall and upstairs. Then she came quickly down again, asked to go out, and disappeared running toward the barn. A few moments later she was back with a kitten in her mouth. I let her in and she took it upstairs and stowed it among files and folders in a far corner of a cupboard in the study.

There was only one kitten, however, and after breakfast Nan found the others dead in the basket, killed in a characteristic manner sometimes adopted by a tomcat where newborn kittens are concerned. We called the survivor Mike. After Annie had had him upstairs for about a week I felt it was time for him to join the family and brought him down one afternoon while Annie was out. He was a fat little ball of long tabby fur with two big eyes in it and a tense little tail sticking straight up. When Annie came in she was furious with me and took him right back upstairs. A week later she brought him down herself, dropped him on the kitchen floor, as good as introduced him to us, then stood by to receive our compliments with fitting modesty and just pride. I think we satisfied her. After that I learned to have eyes in my feet as I worked around the kitchen, for Mike was everywhere. Nor did Dain bother him, her respect for Annie having long since been established by Annie herself.

It was good to get back to our own place after the winter in the studio and it didn't take long to settle in. My husband went right to work on the garden, although it was too early to plant much except peas and onion sets. He also set three broody hens each on a clutch of eggs. The eggs were from our own flock and had presumably been fertilized by the rooster that we had saved from the freezer because of his virile appearance and belligerent behavior. We put him with the hens where he lorded it over them and also over us. On days when my husband was absent and I did barn chores, I had to wear boots when I fed the flock because that rooster would attack my ankles. More than once as he rushed me I caught him with my foot and lifted him across the coop. Perhaps I should have been gentler. In any case, out of all the eggs we set under broody hens that spring, only two proved to be fertile.

Another immediate job was to prepare for the coming of electric power. A neighbor who was an electrician wired the house, the barn, and the cottage while workmen set utility poles in places as unobtrusive as we could persuade them to select. One giant pole at the corner of the barn, however, could not be disguised, and when the men had cut down the small trees that grew near it, it stood forth in all its naked glory as a monument to the modern age. On the day the juice was to be turned on, the electrician wired our kerosene lamps but it took a couple of days for us to drop the habit of approaching a lamp with a match in hand. It was more than a year before we acquired any of the usual electrical household appliances.

The new woodshed had been completed and was big enough to hold the sixteen cords of stove and fireplace wood as planned, plus the car, all the garden and other small tools, and a workbench. The framework of the shed is of big beams sawed out of our own timber. Beams, rafters, and stringers are pegged together in the old style. There is a handy attic overhead. One side of the shed is open under two arches and another is closed only by lattice work to allow the breezes to cure green wood. The whole thing is a masterpiece of workmanship and the architectural proportions turned out just right. Not having enough wood on hand to fill it that spring, we used it for all sorts of other purposes. My husband worked on manuscript there, using a garden table for his typewriter and the wheelbarrow for his books and papers. Once we entertained our guests there at a buffet supper. The workbench became a bar, my husband carved the roast on the wheelbarrow, and we put the salad bowl on the chopping block. Then we sat in garden chairs among the chips and enjoyed a fine early summer evening in what was, in effect, a perfectly good breezeway.

But this was frivolous stuff. A woodshed is serious business, next to the kitchen the most important part of a farm home. It is shop for the man of the family, receiver of many miscellaneous objects that would clutter up the house were they stored inside, and playground of infinite variety for the children. Come fall, the cords of neatly stacked and well-cured firewood that fill the shed are as good as money in the bank.

CHAPTER 7

"Let the Horse Bother"

THE DEEPER WE GOT INTO LIFE ON THE FARM AND BECAME involved in the affairs of the community, the more we realized that the satisfactions thereof stem in part from the special nature of the Vermont character. We had known, from legend and from personal experience, that the Vermont character *is* special. Now we began to understand why. Perhaps, therefore, this as as good a place as any to explode some of the Vermont myths, many of which are based more on the personal idiosyncracies of a famous native son than they are on fact. There is as much diversity of character among Vermonters as elsewhere in the nation. The degree to which the Vermont character differs is the degree to which it has stayed close to the American character as it once was, before it became largely urban and gradually subverted by the softnesses that attend a life of relative ease and luxury compared to what rural areas know.

The Vermont character is many things. It is tough, but sensitive to the point of occasional sentimentality. It is direct, but shrewd and hence capable of an oblique approach. It is simple, but not specialized or narrow and consequently nurtures many interests and abilities. A Vermonter is honest, but he is also a trader and quick to profit from a bargain; consequently he doesn't shrink from that nebulous borderline between the legal and the possibly illegal. He is humorous, but deeply aware of the serious aspects of life in the nuclear age. He is courageous, assuming as a matter of course the presence of courage when needed. But he is also intensely humane and responsive to the hardships of others. He is frugal with money and things, but equally generous with money and things and time.

To sum up the Vermont character, if summary is possible, it might be said that a Vermonter does his own work, makes do with what he has, helps his neighbor, and "lets the horse bother."

The saying "let the horse bother" has a special significance for us as a kind of shorthand description of an aspect of the Vermont character which is otherwise indescribable. It came about this way:

One warm day in spring during World War II when we were driving a horse instead of a car (this was several years prior to permanent residence on the farm), I discovered that one of Judge's front shoes was loose. So after lunch I hitched him to the buggy and drove over to see my friend Lew. Lew was a farmer and blacksmith, but especially he was a philosopher with a marvelous ability to tell a story. A little man of 71 at the time ("Celebrated my 50th wedding anniversary this year and old enough to sign my own marriage license, too," is the way he put it), with sparse hair and hardly any teeth of his own. He had quick bright eyes, a wit, and a depth of human understanding that made him irresistible to all who knew him, including the ladies.

"I never heard that Lew ever did anyone any harm," commented a neighbor to my husband one day when they were working on a job together, "but in his younger days you had to keep a sharp eye on your girl or he'd be toppin' her."

For my part, I loved to call on Lew in his role as blacksmith and listen to him in his role as philosopher and raconteur. I'd sit on an upturned nail keg or sugar bucket in the wide sunny doorway of his smithy and listen to his stories as he worked, now and then, on the hooves of the horse tied in the back part of the shop. Lew would pick up the horse's hoof, look at it, put it down, and begin to tell me a tale about someone who had lived in the neighborhood years ago. He'd fuss around with his tools for a moment, pick up the hoof again, look at it, put it down, and tell me another story. In the end, but after quite a while, the horse would be shod, I would be charged a small fee (as low as a quarter for merely resetting a shoe), and would drive home the richer of the two for the fund of local lore and humor I had gathered and the wonderful leisurely afternoon I had enjoyed sitting in the sun and listening to Lew.

I heard, for example, of the threatened hanging of the former owner of our farm because he was mean to his wife. I heard how the same man would spend the whole day hiding from his family in a ditch in our six-acre lot, chuckling over their discomfiture—or so he supposed—at not being able to find him. (The neighbors, it seems, had a different idea about how the family reacted to the absence of their chief.) I also heard how he used to sit in the front doorway with nothing on but a shirt, to the terror of little boys passing along the road. And how it was rumored that he had a treasure hidden somewhere in the barn. We, of course, have searched the barn ourselves, as have many others before us, but all we've ever found was old whiskey bottles and once, stuffed up over a beam, a woman's old-fashioned blouse with pretty blue and white buttons on it. There might be quite a story in that one.

I also heard how Lew as a young man was responsible for rolling the roads after a heavy snow in the days when snow was not plowed but packed so as to make a proper footing for horse and sleigh. The roller was a huge wooden cylinder perhaps twelve feet in diameter and drawn by two or three teams of horses driven from a seat on the frame. Lew's rig was drawn by six horses which made it hard to negotiate a turn from the road in front of our barn through a narrow gateway into a lane that led up to the quarry property beyond the woods. The roller-and-six often nicked or even knocked down the wooden posts holding the bars that closed the lane when it wasn't in use.

The owner of the farm never failed to become angry (he was noted for his terrible temper) when his posts were damaged, and I doubt if Lew tried too hard to save his feelings. So one day Faber took the old posts out, dug two big holes, set eighteen-inch tree trunks in them, and filled in around with concrete. But he carefully measured the distance between the old posts and set the new ones not an inch farther apart. Lew continued to nick them with his roller, of course, but under the circumstances they stood the strain and probably outlasted the roller.

Years later when my husband was digging in those spots to plant maple saplings, he found the concrete collars. We considered them one of the minor mysteries of our place until Lew's story cleared it up.

I also heard about Lew's Holstein bull, a story that is now

a legend in the neighborhood. This was a large but docile animal that Lew regularly led to water in a neighbor's barnyard across the road. One day as the bull drank at the tub, Lew unwisely turned his back on him to chat with the neighbor over the fence. The bull, suddenly recognizing an unhoped-for opportunity, caught Lew in the seat of his pants and lifted him right over the fence into the road. Lew wasn't hurt except in his feelings and when he recovered from his surprise he managed to regain control of the bull and get him back to his stall.

The next morning, instead of leading the animal out with a chain, Lew used a bull stick snapped into the critter's nose ring. By this time the bull seemed to have got some idea of his own enormous strength and how to use it, and doubtless he was no less independent than his owner. He put his head down and with one horn he "plowed a furrow down the middle of the road," as Lew put it. Then he yanked the ring out of his nose, tearing the flesh and, of course, causing maddening pain. Under its impact he took off and Lew and his neighbor took cover. Toward the end of the morning they were able to chase the bull into the barn and shut him up in a box stall.

After that when the bull was to be used, Lew let the cow onto the barn floor, shut the door, armed himself with a pitchfork, opened the door to the box stall, took cover, and when the bull had performed his function, Lew shooed him back into his stall and barred the door again. When the time came to dispose of the bull because of advancing age, Lew climbed onto a high beam with a rifle, his neighbor opened the door to the box stall, and as the bull came out Lew shot him through the head, thus finally avenging the injury to his dignity and the seat of his pants. Lew kept that skull with a bullet hole in it nailed up in his barn for many years and it is rumored to be still preserved somewhere in the neighborhood.

Lew always varied his stories with accounts of his experiences as a blacksmith, the ornery horses he handled, and the methods he used. It was usually in connection with these tales that his philosophical qualities were best revealed. It was in the course of one of the stories that I learned how one should always "let the horse bother."

On this occasion the horse was a mean one. Each time Lew tried to take up his hoof he moved around, refused to stand, made a fuss, got excited. So Lew put a heavy work harness on him, got his front leg up and suspended it with a strap to the hame on the collar, thus leaving the animal temporarily three-legged. Lew turned him loose in the barnyard and sat on a box and smoked his pipe while the horse staggered around for a while. When Lew thought he'd had enough he released the leg, tied the horse up again beside the anvil, and shod him. This time the horse stood quietly and Lew never again had any trouble with him.

"Always let the horse bother," concluded Lew with a chuckle. Or, translated: if there is any worrying to be done, let the other fellow do it; or at least be sure that it's not you who has to. "Dans la vie," says an old French song, "faut pas s'en faire." The meaning is the same.

Whenever anything went wrong on our place with an animal we always turned to Lew for help and it was always forthcoming. One summer day, for example, a heifer that had had her first calf was so upset by the event that she refused to allow the calf to nurse. For its part the calf, after one or two tries, decided to keep clear of this kicking object that was supposed to be its mother, and wouldn't approach. As greenhorns in the cow stable we were stumped. So my husband went to consult Lew and brought him back with him. Under Lew's direction I stroked the cow's face to soothe her, my husband rubbed the small of her back to relax her hind end, and Lew himself rubbed the calf under its tail to stimulate it's sucking reflexes. The procedure worked and after a few minutes we left mother and calf to their own devices with everything going nicely between them.

A year or so later another first-calf heifer, confused by the approaching birth, ran away from the herd one night and for two days thereafter we combed woods and pastures—our own and those of our neighbors. Once we spotted her with her calf but lost her, and on the following day we caught her but by this time the calf had disappeared. So we consulted Lew.

"I think," he said, "the calf will try to get to the nearest place where there are cows."

And so it proved. We inquired of a neighbor whose herd pastured near our line, if he had seen a calf.

"No," he said, "but some of the cows were kind of excited last night when I drove them in."

Nan searched the pasture and sure enough, there was the calf, several days without food but still fresh enough to give Nan a good chase. She performed a first-rate flying tackle, brought the animal down, and carried her home in her arms. We named her Heidi because she had hid and she grew up to be a pretty good cow; though always, we thought, a little on the wild side.

When he was just a year or so past seventy Lew began to show some personal concern about the onset of old age. One

day when I stopped by his smithy I learned that a mutual
friend who owned the local hardware store had died the day
before at the rather early age of seventy-five. Jim Graham had
been a good friend to all the town, including such newcomers
as ourselves, and I expressed my regret at his passing.

"Yes," said Lew, "I'm sorry too. But the thing that gets
me," he added with a good deal of emphasis, "is that it's
peckin' pretty close to me!"

In the matter of advancing age Lew should have followed
his own advice to let the horse bother. A year or so later he had
trouble with a sore spot in his mouth, it turned out to be
cancer of the jaw, and after a long siege of surgery, X-ray
treatments, and severe pain he won the battle and came back
to shoeing horses.

"They tried to get me," he told me one day when I welcomed him back to the neighborhood, "but they couldn't!"

His face was twisted, his neck scarred, and he could no
longer wear a denture, but his eyes were as bright as ever and
so was his wit. Eventually he sold his farm and moved to a
house in the village but continued to shoe such horses as remained in the area following the introduction of the surplus
army jeep after Word War II. When he finally retired, closer
to ninety than to eighty, he and his wife moved to the local
village hotel and thereafter Lew spent most of his time visiting with his many friends up and down Main Street.

Lew loved good cider and was an able and experienced
judge thereof. When cider and horseshoeing coincided, the
occasion was likely to be an especially happy one for Lew and
for anyone else who chanced to be around. A few years ago
Lew called on us one day as he was passing and we offered
him some of my brother's cider to which Lew accords the

95

profound respect due a beverage made only from wild apples and bottled in the new moon. The last time he had good cider, said Lew, was just the preceding week when he had shod a horse for a man who was new in the neighborhood and whom Lew had not yet met, though he had known the farm through a couple of previous ownerships. There was a nice-looking apple orchard near the barn. When the horse had been shod Lew asked the man if he had had a good apple crop that year. Yes, said the man, he had.

"I thought so," said Lew. "And what did you do with the apples the Lord didn't want?"

"Oh," said the man, "I made cider."

"I thought so," said Lew. "And would you need any help bringing some up from the cellar?"

The man laughed, fetched up a brimming pitcher of cider which, after due sampling, Lew pronounced to be as good as any he'd had in some time. For the rest of the morning, by a good guess, a fine time was had by both, sitting on the side porch and participating in a mutual reaction of cider to anecdote, and Lew in the middle.

* * *

Lew's courage in his successful bout with cancer was remarkable by any of the standards by which most of us would judge it. In the north country such courage is taken for granted, being built into the Vermont character from birth. Life will inevitably have its bad moments; one simply lives through them. A woman past seventy, a neighbor and close friend of ours, once told me how, years before, she had a severe attack of arthritis in her hands and wrists. With all the cooking and

washing she had to do for a large family, she was never without
pain or the need to do things that made the pain worse.

So one morning after breakfast she just took to her bed
and broke down, weeping and sobbing and no doubt thinking
of all the other hardships of her life, and there had been a good
many. Her husband meanwhile—it being Sunday—sat in his
rocking chair near the open door to the bedroom, gently
rocking and reading his paper. One of the boys came in,
noted the distress of his mother, and asked his father what
was wrong with her.

"Your mother," replied his father, in a calm tone with a
hint of reproof in it, "has lost her courage." His wife heard
him, dried her tears, got up, and went about her housework.

It was she also who told me how, soon after she was married,
her husband went to work on the granite quarries that border
our place above the forest. In pre-automobile days quarry
workers lived in the neighborhood. She and her husband rented
what is now the bathroom in our house. When she became
pregnant her husband got permission from the quarry company to build a log cabin on their property. By January it was
ready. The day they moved in, a little pile of snow had accumulated on the floor in the far corner under the bed, and it
stayed there until early April. The baby was born in May,
the first of eight children these two were to have.

By the time the youngest boy was sixteen, the family was
living in a house built by the father just down the road from
the one that became ours. One summer day the youngest
boy hoed the vegetable garden all morning, and since it was
hot, he went down in the afternoon to where the river winds
through the village, to swim with his friends. As he dove into
the water he struck his head on a rock and was killed. Neigh-

bors have told us how neither of the parents showed any emotion at the funeral, but they were never quite the same after that. Many years later, after she had become a widow, the mother told me that there remained in their shed a pile of firewood that the boy had split and that her husband never would disturb or bring into the house.

I've seen this same man, who did not choose to comfort his wife when she lost her courage or to show emotion at the funeral of his son, weep when I read aloud, at his request, a long epic poem of the burning of Chicago in the great fire of 1871. I've seen Lew himself, after his bout with cancer, with tears in his eyes when he told me one day as we stopped our cars on our narrow back road to chat for a moment, how sorry he was to hear that we had lost a baby.

These men and women can face any hardship, can appreciate the effect of hardship on others, and though they are frugal in their own lives and habits, they are correspondingly generous with what they have even if it's only their hands and their time. When a family is burned out, for example, neighbors offer shelter and someone passes a paper around to collect pledges of cash, materials, or labor to rebuild the house or the barn that has been lost. Someone else collects clothing and furniture, if these are needed. If a man is sick, his neighbor feeds his animals and milks his cows morning and night, chops his wood, and even helps get in his hay or his winter wood supply if the illness is a long one.

Just to put all this regard for neighborly helpfulness in its proper perspective, however, it is also true that there are occasional feuds that flare up and quickly become known to everyone in the community. The relationship between two men will smolder for a while, neither likes the other for some reason that probably has more to do with interpersonal chemistry than with character, there are a few preliminary clashes, and then one day some small matter (in one case it was the price of a shovel handle) triggers off a full-fledged feud, though without the physical deadliness of the variety reputed to flourish in the mountains of Kentucky.

In Vermont a feud sometimes means little more than the cessation of social intercourse between the two families. If they happen to attend the same community gathering, each acts as though the other were not there. The matter may also extend to backbiting and as many little meannesses as either side feels it can get away with in the judgment of the public. Perhaps something also depends on the extent to which a man's system can produce a sufficiently continuous flow of adrenalin to keep the animosity alive until it is finally buried in the respective graves of both parties to it.

A Vermonter is usually a direct sort of person, saying what he thinks as plainly as he can without, except deliberately, hurting another person's feelings. He is also a born trader with a quick eye for a bargain, and here other qualities are called for. My friend Lew, for example, was as sharp a trader as any. He made it a rule, however, never to bargain with a woman because in bargaining no holds are barred, which he considered unchivalrous where money and women are concerned. (Where women only are concerned, of course, that's something else again, and Lew was quite an expert in that field, too.)

If a Vermonter's opposite number in a trade is unwary or unsophisticated in local customs and mores, and especially if he is an out-of-stater setting himself up as a country gentleman and hiring all his work done for him, then he is tacitly declared fair game and anything goes. But even among friends, when a trade is in course, each party to it must be wary lest he get the short end of the deal. He who gets the better of a friend in a bargain may do so regretfully, but a trade is a trade and a bargain not something to be half-hearted about unless to win would cause a real injustice. And even then . . . .

* * *

Although a Vermonter is usually a simple man in the best sense of the term—in his directness, his honesty, his frugality, and his realism—he is not a narrow man in his abilities or interests or in his concern for the welfare of his fellowmen or even of mankind. He reads, especially during the winter months when his farm work has slowed down to barn chores and keeping up the wood supply. He follows the news with keen interest and curiosity and passes on it with a down-to-earth kind of judgment. One of the most alert people I know in our community is a little lady on the far side of seventy who can argue on the subject of Tito, for example, with a high degree of sophistication. The fiscal policy of the New Deal, said a Vermonter to me one day during that era, seemed fantastic at first glance, but viewed as a whole it appeared to follow the course of a sailing vessel that tacks first one way and then the other in its course toward a particular destination. This was an accurate analysis, as a good many have since agreed. The public interest is the passionate interest of many Vermonters and the care with which local and state politicians treat it does much to determine their political future.

On town-meeting day, divisions of opinion are often sharp and sometimes even bitter, but each side has the public interest at heart and disagrees only as to how best to serve it. Shall we build a new high school or make do with the old one a little longer? A new one will be expensive and Vermonters are characteristically against debt. There is already the debt for the new water system, installed a few years ago to replace one that had been patched to the point of imminent breakdown. But there are the needs of the children to consider, too. Perhaps we should join with a neighboring town to build a union high school. But then we lose some of our independence. Each point is argued with an intensity that is almost passionate. The final vote is to build our own school. The decision pleases those who fought for it but both sides are sobered by the thought of the debt that will be incurred. And both sides now go to work to build as fine a school as they can.

A Vermonter doesn't like, as the saying is, to be "curried below the hocks." Anyone who has ever curried a horse will understand the reference. The area below the hocks has very little flesh on it, the bone is close to the surface, the hair lies flat on the skin. A curry is a hard instrument that feels good in the right place but below the hocks it pulls the hair the wrong way and pinches what flesh there is against the bone— altogether an irritating experience and no horse worth his salt will stand for it.

A Vermonter will do what he must even if it means going into debt, but he doesn't like to be pushed into it. He must be free to make his own decisions. If he chooses to make them on the basis of his personal sense of values, which may not jibe with those of his fellows, that's his right and he insists on it. In some ways he's a little like his own Morgan horse, according to an analysis I once heard from an ex-jockey who lived in our neighboring village.

This man was little and old and bent with rheumatism, but he had a twinkle in his eye and a quiet way with horses. He loaned me his racing saddle one day—I needed a saddle and that was the only one there was that Lew could think of in the neighborhood—but when I wanted to buy it Charlie said no, he was "sort of fond of it" and wanted to keep it. At the time, we owned a temperamental mare called Jenny who looked as though she were part Morgan. She had been mistreated and was hard to manage.

"Well," said Charlie, "with a Morgan you have to be just so. If you go up to her stall in the morning and tip your hat nice and polite and say, 'Good morning, lady, and would you mind moving over just a little so I can come in?' she'll move over sweet as anything. But if you go up to her and say, 'Get the hell over there,' she'll kick you right out of the stall. And a good thing, too."

Perhaps this is the place to refute the myth of chilly taciturnity saddled on Vermonters by way of the Coolidge myth. If taciturnity means keeping your mouth shut until you have something to say or until you've sized up a stranger, perhaps Vermonters *are* taciturn. There is the story of the son of a Vermonter returning to his father's town that he left many years ago and where now he isn't known. He greets a man working on the sidewalk of the village street with the comment that it seems like a nice day, and gets no reply. He asks about that house over there where his father used to live. The man looks at him briefly but still doesn't speak. But when the stranger remarks that his grandfather had also lived in that house, the man on the sidewalk straightens up and gives him a good look.

"Well," he says. "Guess it might be a nice day at that."

This story could well be true and the appearance of taciturnity still be wholly superficial. Vermonters size people up quickly according to a few simple criteria (Do they do their own work? Do they pay their bills? Can they take a joke?) and after that there always seems to be a good deal to say. Indeed, "visiting" is a popular pastime in these hills, whether it be over the phone (sometimes a three- or four-way conversation over the party line), or as neighbors encounter each other in their cars on a back road, or as one stops to pass the time of day with you if he sees you in your yard, or as you go to the barber, the local lunch room, or the grocery store. So, far from taciturnity on such occasions there is, rather, a loquacity of no mean order. A certain friendliness is universal. On the score of warmth, I don't think I've ever encountered a Vermonter who was chilly in his relations with other people unless, of course, it happened to be someone he was feuding with.

Time is something else that people in the north country seem to understand better than most. There is a certain aspect of time that is more readily appreciated in a rural area, which Vermont still largely is. Thus, a Vermonter is usually a hard worker and moves quickly, yet he's seldom in a hurry. I once remarked to Lew that so-and-so always seemed to be terribly busy.

"Yes," said Lew. "That's so. He is. But, you know, some people can be awfully busy and not get much done." I realized at once that this particular individual seldom did get things done in any systematic way, while Lew, for his part, always had plenty of time even when he was most busy.

Once during the war when we were driving a horse instead of a car, I made the trip home from town the long way round so as to stop at a certain farm to pick up a couple of chickens for the Sunday pot.

"It'll take a little time to get them ready," said the farmer, "and I expect you're in a hurry."

"No," I replied, without even thinking about it, "with a horse and buggy you can't be in a hurry."

And so it is. You gear your life to a leisurely pace—a trip to town once a week instead of every day or so. And in a buggy your mind is free to wander over all kinds of subjects while your horse goes quietly about his business and takes all morning to do it.

Some of the loveliest occasions I can remember were spent in a buggy while driving at a deliberate pace between home and town, especially at night or very early in the morning. I recall, for example, getting up at three o'clock one spring morning, hitching the horse by lanternlight, and, while it was still dark, driving the five miles to the station to meet my husband on the early train from New York. The silence of the back road, a little foggy here and there in the bottoms, with the feel of dew all around, the farm houses along the way still dark, and the occasional chirp of a bird disturbed by the passage of the rig or just waking up: these things I remember.

Then there was the warm, still summer night that, after taking my husband to the midnight train for a trip to the city, I drove Jenny home in the moonlight. There wasn't a breath of breeze and I became aware of certain smells dominating certain stretches of the road. It was like passing through a series of zones, each with a different odor, my nose telling me just when we left one and entered the next. In one zone there was the smell of pines, then it was ferns, in a woody section it was humus, a rotting log, then a farmyard, then a pond, then a hilltop where a fugitive breeze had got all the smells mixed up together. Quiet horse-and-buggy experiences such as these were once more common even in Vermont than they are now but something of their flavor is still part of the Vermont character.

*　　*　　*

In addition to being direct, hard-working, down to earth, and concerned with the public interest—all of which are pretty solemn things—most Vermonters also have a sense of humor that is seldom contrived. Or if it is, it is done so openly and with such gusto that the contriving itself becomes part of the joke.

The owner of the local hardware store quickly became a good friend of ours, as he was a good friend to all the town, and took an interest in our buying and restoring our place. When our house burned he was greatly distressed; a day or so later when I went in to buy some nails he wouldn't let me pay for them, insisting also on offering me, as a token of his sympathy, some item of his wares that might be useful to me. He wanted to make it a kitchen utensil but I chose a whisk broom, which was what I needed at the moment. (I used it for years, until nearly all the whisks were gone, then burned it in the kitchen stove with a final thought of gratitude.)

One day I went to buy a thermometer at Mr. Graham's store, which was old and a little disorderly with an untidy old roll-top desk in a back corner near a window that overlooked the railroad tracks. Mr. Graham came forward to wait on me. What kind of thermometer did I want, indoor or outdoor?

"An outdoor one," I said.

"Well," said Mr. Graham, "we only have the kind that goes down to 50° below zero."

It had actually been that cold for a couple of days during the preceding winter. I said that was the kind I needed, all right. I am glad to report, however, that the instrument I bought has never been put to the test for which Mr. Graham said it was prepared. Minus 36° is about as low as the temperature has ever dropped while we've been on the farm.

Once, after we had rebuilt the house, I was staying there alone for a while doing inside painting, which is always best accomplished without family around. When it came time to return to the city, a neighbor offered to take me to the midnight train. He arrived on schedule, I got in the car, and as he slid behind the wheel he let forth a most majestic belch.

"Had some cabbage for supper," he commented shortly. "Just as soon it went the other way now."

On another occasion he was standing in his doorway one morning when a friend came up the hill on foot with an ax over his shoulder on his way to work up some cordwood.

"Hello, Charlie," said our friend. "Goin' to chop down some trees?"

"Heh, heh," said the man with the ax. "Goin' to chop some down and goin' to chop some up. Heh, heh." And without pausing in his stride he marched on up the hill, chuckling at his own wit.

Much Vermont humor is a matter of understatement, which makes it the more delicious. There is the story (apocryphal, perhaps) of how a man who had never got on with his mother-in-law was required to be present one day at the exhuming of her body. Neighbors in a high state of curiosity asked him how she looked.

"Mighty peaked," was his only reply.

Similarly, on a broiling summer day, two truck drivers were resting in the shade bordering the unloading area of a small barrel factory. In the area itself an elderly man was methodically and apparently unconcernedly raking gravel. The truck drivers commented to him on the heat two or three times before he finally paused in his work for a moment and remarked,

"Yes . . . I guess it has thawed some."

Sometimes understatement is carried to the point of no statement at all, merely an attitude. One such incident occurred at an auction sale put on for a benefit, the auctioneer donating his services for the evening. The various contributed items were put up, knocked down to the high bidder, and transferred to their new owners in the hall. Finally there came a pair of potted cactus plants of the kind that is composed of long, dark green, sectioned branches. I think they are sometimes called Christmas cactus but these were not the big beautiful ones that many of us know; neither plant had more than two or three long branches. One plant seemed fairly chipper but the other was obviously *in extremis*, its two long limp green branches hanging lifelessly, almost obscenely, over the side of the pot in a most distressing way.

Bob held it up and looked at it, then looked at the audience, and the audience began to laugh. Bob joined it, quietly as befitted his official position as auctioneer, while mirth flowed from side to side and up and down the hall in waves. Finally someone bid a nickel.

"You've bought it!" said Bob, and added, "Thank God."

I think the masterpiece of all Vermont understatement was related to me by our friend George who, one fine Sunday in spring, took his family for a drive up into the hills in search of a road that would take them over the mountain to the neighboring town. Many of these small roads have been abandoned, or thrown up, as the term is, and this one fetched up in the dooryard of an old house. On the porch, a man was sitting back in a chair, taking his ease in fine solitude. George leaned out of the car and called to him:

"Does this road go through to Rochester?"

The man shook his head.

"Well," said George, "then I guess I'm lost."

A nod from the porch. That was all. George turned the car and drove off.

A final story shows how the Vermont humor may be used to achieve more than mirth. A man who lived alone on the edge of a village began to notice that firewood was disappearing from his shed. He had an idea who might be taking it, so one night he put his light out as usual but sat by his kitchen window to see what would happen. Sure enough, after a while a man came across the adjoining field, went into the shed, came out with an armload of wood, and started back across the field. So the owner of the wood also went into the shed, gathered an armload, followed his neighbor across the field, through his shed, and into his kitchen. The neighbor dumped his wood into the box behind his stove and the owner of the wood also dumped his load into the box. Then, dusting his hands one against the other, he remarked;

"There, I guess that'll hold you 'til morning."

A second version of the same story has it that the thief took dry wood from his neighbor's shed, the neighbor followed him with an armload of green wood, and when he dumped it into the box behind the stove his comment was,

"There, damn it, burn that too. I have to."

*   *   *

I realize that I am open to criticism for recording here only the better things about the north country character, and I must admit the truth of the charge. There is, of course, the other side of the picture, in Vermont as elsewhere, though perhaps less than elsewhere so far. (Here is my prejudice showing again). There is the increasing effect, for example—especially among young people—of a fast, shiny, brittle modern culture (if that is what it is) impinging on Americans everywhere and, indeed, following everywhere in the world that Americans go.

If I have not considered the effect of this trend in Vermont it is because I don't want to. I and many others are sentimental about the state we live in, to the point where we have become a byword among our neighbors from other states. If justification is needed for so soft an attitude, I can only submit that in a world that seems to be headed toward automation, toward the cut-and-dried and the predetermined, a little spontaneous and perfectly harmless sentiment not inspired by the idiot box is a good thing. It is perhaps an additional sign of the times that I find myself feeling defensive about it.

CHAPTER 8

Professor, Author,
Farmer, Politician

IT WAS ON RETURNING TO OUR OWN PLACE AFTER THE WINTER
in Mom's studio that my husband added to the list of his occupations as reported on his income tax return. A leading
citizen of Bethel asked him if he would be willing to run for
the office of town representative in the state legislature. All
he had to do was to declare Bethel as his legal residence and
take the Freeman's Oath.

He had served in several administrative jobs in Washington, and as a professor of government he liked the idea of
serving also in a legislative body. We didn't plan to write
another book that year, so he would have time for the session,
which would run from the following January through most of
the spring. Time was when the sessions of the Vermont
General Assembly were concluded by March in order to allow
the members to go home for sugaring, but the pressure of the
public business was making each one a little longer than the
last. The pay was low and probably would not cover expenses

but we were getting some fancy royalties from our first text-book so the financial aspect of the matter seemed all right. It meant the boss would be away from home except on week-ends but I was prepared to carry on with Nan as chief assistant, so that was all right, too.

From my husband's standpoint the main objection to run-ning for office was the need, as he supposed, to conduct a campaign. He likes to speak in public and does it well but he is not persuasive where his own interests are concerned. He was assured, however, that a personal campaign would not be necessary. His friends would conduct one for him. In a small town, a political campaign is largely by word of mouth anyway. It was felt that as a farmer and tree planter most of his support would come from the rural section of the town and that he would be an able speaker for men who are not normally very articulate.

There were other points in his favor. It was known, for example, that he had once, singlehanded, spread twelve truck-loads of cow manure in one day, pitching on and off with only a barn fork. It was also known that we did our own work, hiring only what we couldn't do ourselves—such as expert carpentry and stone masonry—and that I had never had outside help in the house.

The question of political affiliation was a little more com-plicated because my husband's convictions on that score were largely unknown. Vermonters are deeply concerned over party politics in state and national elections. For local office, how-ever, the candidate is known to most people personally and this is often considered more important than the party label he bears. As a young man my husband had registered as a Republican but after he became a teacher of government it seemed proper to take a neutral stand in public and thereafter his personal preferences were discussed only in private.

On the other hand, it was well known in the community that most of his work in Washington had been during the New Deal period and that at the time we bought our place he was Assistant Secretary of Labor in FDR's "little cabinet." This seemed to indicate to our neighbors that he might have been at least partially subverted by the Democratic party, and at that time Democrats were a good deal scarcer in Vermont than they are today. Consequently when the matter of political affiliation was finally broached, both parties to the conversation were a little tentative.

"You *are* a Republican, I suppose?" was the question when it finally came. My husband hesitated, which seemed to be the answer, and the question was considerately rephrased:

"Or anyhow, you're a Republican in Vermont, aren't you?"

"Yes," replied my husband, "I guess that's right."

Both men laughed and the matter was settled.

The primary election was to be held in September and since there would be no Democratic opposition in November, the outcome of the primary would be decisive. A few days later we both took the Freeman's Oath. An American citizen, says the Vermont constitution, who has resided in the state for a year before the election of representatives, "and who is of a quiet and peaceable behavior," is entitled "to all the privileges of a freeman of this state" if he will take the following oath or affirmation:

You solemnly swear (or affirm) that whenever you give your vote or suffrage, touching any matter that concerns the State of Vermont, you will do it so as in your conscience you shall judge will most conduce to the best good of the same, as established by the Constitution, without fear or favor of any person.

Each of us raised our right hand and solemnly took this oath as administered by the town clerk, and a record of it was made in his big book. Thereafter—and ever since—we have been fully qualified freemen in the state in which we have chosen to make our home.

*   *   *

Meanwhile there was the summer's work to be done. The garden grew well, vegetables were gathered and stored in the freezer, berries were picked in their season and what remained after pies and shortcakes also went to the freezer. Then we put a pig in it and examined the herd for an unlikely looking heifer for the same destination. Unlikely, that is, as a future milker. Our beef was always a cull animal.

Unfortunately all the heifers looked pretty good that year so my husband cast his eye on the bull, an animal we had used in the herd for several years. He had been born in our pasture, a husky, sassy little calf, and we learned the meaning of the verb "to hightail" by watching him streak across the pasture with his tail straight up in the air. Because he was light and quick we called him Deerfoot but he rapidly outgrew the connotation and in a year or so was a good deal more powerful than he was quick.

He was now five years old, which is about the limit of usefulness even for a registered bull—as this animal was—unless one is willing to keep detailed records to prove his worth through the milk production of his daughters. We weren't prepared to do this so Deerfoot was marked for the freezer. I demurred on the ground that he was old and would be tough.

"Nonsense," said my husband. "The Greeks always preferred the meat of a mature bull because it is tasty and virile-making," or words to that effect.

So in due course our friend was dressed off and presented to me, quarter by quarter, each one almost too big to be accommodated on my cutting table in the pantry. There were nearly a hundred pounds of hamburg in the neck alone, and the bones yielded forty quarts of soup stock. I had not misjudged the toughness of the meat, however, though my husband was right about its flavor and presumably also about its virility-generating potential.

By accident, I found a remedy for the toughness. I had once tried to make elderberry wine, but bottled it before the fermentation was complete and the result was popping corks and spilled wine on the cellar floor. This summer I tried again and went to the other extreme, waiting so long before bottling that the juice had turned to vinegar. But such vinegar! The most acid brew I've ever tasted, with a winy flavor that was good. It occurred to me that it would make a good tenderizer for the bull meat, and so it proved. A pot roast cooked slowly with half a cup of elderberry vinegar turned out to be a very tasty dish to set before the boss.

An earlier experiment in the home-prepared meat line had not turned out so well and I still feel a little frustrated about it. We had dressed off a young heifer and I had asked that the stomach be saved along with the liver and heart and kidneys because I wanted to try to make tripe. Both my husband and I like it very much. I'd never seen a cow's stomach before, however, and when it was presented to me it turned out to be a large, involuted, rough-looking object, a cross between an old doormat that the dogs have been worrying and a mess of wet hay. It was big, thick, tough, shapeless, and brownish-green. A remarkable organ.

Inquiring of the local butcher, who in turn had to inquire of the local Italian colony, I found that the first job was to clean this thing. Being awkward to handle and full of pockets (a cow's stomach is really seven stomachs) cleaning it presented many difficulties. I took it to the brook and let the water run over it while I scrubbed, but that seemed a long and at best incomplete job. So then I tied a rope to one corner of it and dropped it over the spillway of the dam into a kind of well that leads into a culvert under the road, tying the other end of the rope to a spike in the side of the spillway. The water falling from some height did seem to begin to do the job so I left the thing there for a while.

Other duties claimed my attention, however, and also the weather turned hot. A few days later a group of neighbors—city people they were, too—came to swim in the pond. One of the girls, being curious about the rope hitched to the spillway, pulled it up, and along came the would-be tripe. There was quite a commotion. After that my husband buried the remains under the rhubarb and I decided to buy my tripe at the store.

*   *   *

One important event for us that summer was based on the sheerest coincidence.

We had wanted to buy a lot in the little cemetery that lies at the point where our back road joins the blacktop. On inquiry we learned that no lot was available. A block of five lots was vacant but the owner had apparently forgotten about them and no one knew where he was. Then on a quiet sunny morning in July a car stopped in front of our house and a quick, elderly little lady came to our door. She was small and erect and sort of simple and direct, with an air of being in command of the situation.

"I wonder," she asked, "if I might look around here just a little. You see," she explained, "I was born in this neighborhood. I'm visiting for a few days in Royalton and I don't suppose I shall be back here again." Her tone was matter-of-fact, but the allusion was plain.

Then she told me her name and where she was born and lived until she was fourteen when her father took the family to Montana. Her grandfather—or maybe it was her father—had come to Vermont from Connecticut, built the house and settled the farm that adjoins ours on the far south side. He had brought with him a bag of apple seed and planted the first orchard on Christian Hill. As a child this lady had gone to school in a one-room schoolhouse, walking cross-lots through pastures in all kinds of weather. She remembered each farm in the neighborhood and asked who lived there now, and in turn related bits and pieces of her memories of those who had formerly lived there.

"But what I really came to do in Bethel," she said finally, "was to bury my sister. We lived together for years and she died this summer and I had her ashes with me."

When she arrived in town she had tried to find the sexton but he was away, and since it was noon, the town clerk's office was closed.

"So I just went up to the cemetery and buried her myself," she told me. "I had a shovel in the car and I knew right

where the lot was." As it turned out, it was one of the
mysterious five. She laughed a little and went on:

"The next day I went back to the town clerk's office and
told him what I'd done and he was scandalized. He wanted
to know if I had a burial permit and I told him that it said
on the package, 'Burial Permit Inside.' So of course there was
a permit."

Apparently this wasn't enough for the town clerk, however;
he called in the sexton and the whole thing became quite
complicated while the little lady sat quietly by and smiled to
herself at the ways of town officials.

"Look," she asked them finally, "can't I just sign something?"

But that suggestion also seemed to be a shocking one. In
telling about it she was amused all over again. Such a simple
thing, after all, just to take your own shovel and bury your
own sister in your own cemetery lot, with no fuss or bother.
I fully agreed with her, and let the bureaucracy simmer.

Then we got to talking about the Abbott Lot, which is an
area of maybe forty acres bordering our land beyond the forest
to the north. This lot was a source of continual interest and
mystery to us, for abandoned as it now was, it had once been
the center of a thriving community surrounding the granite
quarries located on the ridge above it. Known as Bethel White
because it is more white than grey, the stone from this quarry
is of a superior quality and has been used in the construction
of a number of prominent buildings including the state capitol
at Madison, Wisconsin, part of the Cathedral of St. John the
Divine in New York, and in Washington the Union Station,
the New Post Office, and part of the Smithsonian Institution.

In the days when the quarry was in full operation, this company employed several hundred workmen. There were the stone cutters, mostly Italians, as well as blacksmiths, wheelwrights, cartwrights, teamsters, carpenters, masons, harnessmakers, and machinists. To accommodate these men there was a boardinghouse close by and a group of makeshift cottages favored by the Italians. In addition, most of the farmhouses in the neighborhood also boarded workmen and their families. At one time there were 33 people living in the house that became ours and 11 in the four-room cottage across the road. To provision these people, traveling purveyors of meat, vegetables, bread, and clothing made regular rounds through the quarry community.

My visitor knew many of these people including the Lewis Abbotts. Their homestead was the closest to the quarry and became the center of the community. Lewis Abbott was a man of strength, imagination, kindness, and public spirit. He was also a fruit-fancier and set out around his homestead a variety of fruit trees including apples, plums, pears, peaches, and cherries; except for the apples, these are all hard to grow at this latitude. Lilacs, a snowball bush, and bush honeysuckle grew in his door yard, together with a mass of cinnamon roses. Mrs. Abbott was a fine cook and workers were eager to board at her house. A big barn stabled some of the great horses that hauled the granite.

That was the situation when the quarry operation was on the upgrade, and when the downgrade set in, toward the end of the 1920s, it went very quickly. The granite was expensive and the market declined. Contracts were hard to get and workers were laid off. Some half-wit set fire to the Abbott barn and it wasn't rebuilt. Mrs. Abbott died and Lewis started to build a house on the road below what was to be our place, but he died before it was well under way. In grief and respect, his neighbors erected a granite watering trough at the side of the road in front of the abandoned cellar hole, and put his name on it. His own house was sold for the materials it contained and was dismantled.

My visitor was eager to know what the Abbott Lot looked like now and I told her. The mass of cinnamon roses, a huge lilac tree, the snowball bush, and wild berry bushes have grown over the foundations of the house. Only a square of huge stones shows where the barn once stood. The more delicate of the fruit trees have died but the apple trees remain and so does a big crab apple tree that grows beside what was once the front door. Deer are fond of apples and the Abbott Lot is a wonderful refuge for them when food is scarce. Second growth is pushing up in the fields, and in late summer the goldenrod is as tall as a man. It is a good place for berrying, for picnics, and for dreaming in the sun.

At the quarry itself in our day, only the boardinghouse, the great derricks of Douglas Fir, and abandoned machinery were left. During World War II a junk company bought the remains, the derricks were hauled off for lumber and the machinery and the steel hawsers for scrap. A family was living in the boardinghouse but one day as my husband and I were working in the garden we saw a mass of dense smoke billow up suddenly over the hill that separates us from the quarry. It could only be the boardinghouse going up in flames and it was too late to do anything about it except help to collect what was needed for the burned-out family.

After that, all was quiet on the quarry hillside for a number of years. Although nature had done its usual efficient job and covered all the scars made by man, it never could conceal the mountains of waste granite (called grout) that stand out against the green of the hillside where it was dumped. Nor could anything conceal the two great excavated pits which are endlessly fascinating to us. Sharp and white, with giant steps made by the quarried layers of granite, they look like something the gods might have put together. The lower pit has a little water in it but the upper one is full to the brim and offers a wonderful swim in the warm sunshine. Bits of rusted steel hawser, a few spikes, a rotting length of Douglas Fir testify to the presence of many men where today the summer quiet is broken only by the croak of a bullfrog. In the fall the bright colors stand out sharply against the white granite. But loveliest and most mysterious of all is the winter landscape in a light snow, a study in black and grey and white, and not a sound anywhere except the faint impact of falling snow when the flakes are a little wet.

My visitor was deeply interested in what I had to tell her and asked if she might come back some other day and pick berries in the Abbott Lot. But of course, I said; she would be most welcome. Then she got in her car and said goodbye and drove off slowly up the hill toward town.

A few days later she was back, wearing a pair of faded blue cotton slacks, an old shirt and sweater, and rubbers, and carrying a basket with her lunch in it. She greeted me cheerily, said that the business about burying her sister was all straightened out now, and went happily off into the woods. Several hours later she returned looking a little weary but satisfied.

"I've had a wonderful day," she said. "And look at all the berries I've picked!" Her basket was full of wild raspberries.

"Unfortunately," she added, "I lost one of my rubbers. But no matter. It was an old pair."

She put her basket in the car and picked up a small package that was on the seat.

"Grass seed," she said. "I disturbed the sod a little in the cemetery and I'm just going to stop by and scatter some seed on it." She settled herself behind the wheel.

"I won't be back," she said. "Goodbye, and thank you." With that she drove off, slowly as before; I never did see her again.

Shortly afterward we learned that she had turned back to the cemetery association three unused burial lots and that we might have one of them if we liked. We did like. And a couple of years later while picking wild raspberries in the Abbott Lot, I found her rubber among the bushes surrounding the foundations of the old house which she must have known as a proper dwelling when she was a little girl. I left the rubber where I found it as a kind of monument, trivial to the eye but to me full of meaning to the memory of a gallant lady.

*   *   *

As the summer drew to a close, local interest in the September primary elections increased somewhat, but not much. Often enough in Vermont's small town elections there is only one candidate for the office of town representative, and generally it is the man or woman best able to spare the time for it. This year, however, there were two candidates on the Republican ticket and hence a bit of rivalry to enliven the situation. There were no Democratic candidates. My husband made only one speech—to a small neighborhood group on the far side of the township—and I don't think his rival made any. Primary day arrived, ballots were cast throughout the day at the town hall, and when the tally was in, my husband had

20969

won the contest. (Later when he was required by law to report the figure for his campaign expenses, it amounted to the price of a three-cent stamp; I don't remember the purpose for which it was used.)

Now our plans for the winter had to include not only the farm but also part-time residence at Montpelier for my husband. Nan was to enter high school in Bethel. Mark had decided to take the course at the Aggie school at Randolph Center, a village five miles away. He would live with us some of the time but mostly at school. On the farm there was a new farm operator and the usual barn full of cows. At the center of these activities I would try to coordinate the various family comings and goings that would be necessary, take care of Davis, do our share of the barn chores (pigs and chickens), read proof on the new textbook, and revise the first one, which by now had been three years in print and was due for a new edition. I would also keep an eye on Mom who was planning to spend the winter on her own place this year. My youngest sister, Betty, who was an arthritic cripple, was with her and so was my sister Sidney, who would look after the two of them.

I like barn chores. There's something pleasant and satisfying about taking care of animals. Our pig was a sow called Emma and it was her brother who was in the freezer. She was purebred Yorkshire which means she was long and lean, a producer of the highest-grade pork. Her winter quarters would be in the barn and we wondered how to get her there from her pen by the brook. A pig is an awkward animal to get a grip on. It has no neck to speak of, so you can't just put a rope around it and lead the beast. A pig won't lead anyway unless it is willing to cooperate and you can't count on that. Nor can you drive a pig in any way that assures control over its direction; and this pig, at any rate, was too big to be carried, even on the wheelbarrow.

So we did a little research among our neighbors and learned that, sure enough, this farm problem too had its solution. If you put a bucket over a pig's face and head, you can *back* the animal from one place to another. So we tried it on Emma, to her audible indignation but with success on our part. And a ridiculous sight it was, too: a huge protesting sow being slowly backed a hundred yards or so with a bucket over her face and a determined professor pushing on the bottom of it, with his wife on the sidelines ready (she hoped) for any emergency.

After that we bred Emma to a Chester White boar; she would farrow sometime during the following May.

My husband then arranged winter quarters for the chickens in another part of the barn. The pullets were beginning to lay. As the eggs accumulated beyond our daily needs I preserved them in water glass in big crocks in the cellar. It began to look as though whatever else might happen, at least we wouldn't starve.

The next job was to fill the new woodshed, which had stood virtually empty all summer. My husband loves to work in the woods and with the help of a neighbor he got out something like fifteen cords of firewood that fall. This was before the days of the chain saw—on our farm, at any rate—and the only tools were the crosscut saw, the ax, and a set of wedges. Trees are cut down, their branches trimmed off, the trunks and the larger limbs sawed into four-foot lengths, the thicker pieces split with splitting ax and wedges, and then it is all piled. Later the logs are hauled down to the house, cut with a buzz saw into stove- and fireplace-lengths, and tossed into a great pile in the shed.

After that my job is to sort the wood according to its future use in cookstove, chunk stove, or fireplace, and stack it in rows reaching to the ceiling. I seem to be the only member of the family with an eye capable of perceiving balance in physical things; without balance a stack of piled wood quietly becomes a booby trap to the unwary. It settles, it leans, it sags, finally it falls.

This wasn't the first time we'd had occasion to reflect on the wisdom of the Lord in providing wood as a warmer of the human body. Each time wood is handled it stimulates the circulation—and it is handled often: cut, trim, saw, split, stack, haul, saw, toss, stack, and finally carry it into the house. No wonder that when you sit before an open fire burning wood that by now you know so well, there is a special kind of satisfaction in the heat that comes directly instead of—as up to now—indirectly from it.

A final need was to make the house winterworthy. We knew well enough that it was not. Even though the brick walls are solid enough and the frame part is insulated, windows in an old house seldom fit tightly and even when they do, single windows offer little protection against sub-zero weather and a brisk wind. This house had never had storm windows and I can only imagine what a windy day in winter must have felt like even in the kitchen. Once, several years earlier, I had spent from February to early May on the farm with only a dog for company while my husband was finishing a job in Washington, and I had had a fine opportunity to judge of these matters at first hand.

So now we bought a full set of storm windows and painted, cleaned, and hung them. Hanging them turned out to be a rather hazardous job because two gable windows are very

high, two dormers are hard to reach except from pretty far
to the side, and the ladder is long and heavy and awkward to
handle even by the two of us. Holes for screws had to be
drilled by hand in the frames of the new windows and those
of the old ones. I held the foot of the ladder while my husband
exerted himself at the top of it as it swayed alarmingly under
his weight. I also had to hand up tools and retrieve those that
fell when he suddenly found he needed three hands. He is
no lightweight and I worry about his engaging in acrobatics
on a steep roof between ladder and dormer window. I also
worry about the effects of his frustrated lefthandedness and
was glad enough when the job was done.

Next we piled old hay around the foundations of the house
to keep the frost out of the cellar (banking, this operation is
called) and laid new evergreen boughs on top of the hay for
looks, though it would be covered with snow soon enough and
look even better. Finally, we had the chimneys cleaned and
then set up a chunk stove in the living room to one side of the
fireplace so we could use both if we wanted to.

What more could we do to prepare for this first winter in
our own house? We figured this was just about it. With a full
freezer, full cellar bins and pantry shelves, a full shed of wood,
and a house as tight as we could make it, we looked forward
with some degree of confidence to whatever the winter might
bring.

CHAPTER 9

Legislative Winter

THERE IS A SAYING IN THE NORTH COUNTRY THAT A FARM woman goes to church so as to have a chance to sit down. This seems an interesting commentary on the endlessness of woman's work, but I had never appreciated the truth of it in a personal way until my husband departed for the session of the state legislature at Montpelier. After that I acquired an understanding of the need for rest, at least on Sunday, that was very personal indeed. I look back on that winter of 1949 as the hardest I've ever lived through and it took most of the following summer to recover from it.

My usual day started at 5:30 when I got up while it was still dark and cold, restored fires, started breakfast, and then, while Nan dressed Davis and made her lunch, I took care of the pig and the chickens. This meant lugging two pails of hot water to the barn. With one I made Emma a warm mash. I also gave her fresh hay for bedding and saw that she was as comfortable as possible in her dark little pen under the runway to the haybarn. There was no electricity in her quarters and I had to use a flashlight. With the second pail of hot water I thawed out the drinking fountain in the chicken pen and made the hens a warm mash. Then I refilled their drinking fountain, added grain to the food hopper and litter to the floor if it was needed. There were lights in this part of the barn, which made it easier and somehow warmer than tending the pig at that hour of the morning.

Back at the house, breakfast would be ready, and after we had eaten, Nan would get Davis into his snowsuit and collect her gear while I tried to start the car. For the most part it did pretty well. Then the three of us would head for town, pick up the daughter of a neighbor on the way, and arrive at school in time for the opening bell—unless, of course, the Olds was moody and we spent part of the time getting it out of a ditch.

After leaving the girls I would do the shopping and get back to the farm by about 9:30. I would tie a short length of sleigh bells around Davis' waist and send him out with Dain, then do the dishes and make the beds, and by 10 o'clock would be at work upstairs in the study. With a fire in the chunk stove, my papers spread out on the big double desk, the sun stream- ing in at the south window, and a lovely clear view out over the snow-covered pasture, the study was a pleasant place in which to work and I always enjoyed it. Every now and then I'd listen for the sound of Davis' bells and so knew where he was without having to leave my work to check on him.

The work consisted of revising the American government textbook for a forthcoming new edition and putting through proof and indexing the textbook we'd written at the studio the preceding winter. This meant that sheafs of galley proof, fol- lowed by masses of page proof, were coming in and had to be read and corrected and sent off again at once, thus interrupting the revision of the earlier book. There were additional inter-ruptions, of course, to collect eggs from the barn at noon, prepare and eat lunch, put Davis down for his afternoon nap, get him up again an hour later, and finally knock off for good at about 3:30 to go to town to fetch Nan and Jeanne, although they sometimes came home with a neighbor which relieved me of that chore.

Nan's first job when she got home was to split wood and fill the woodboxes for cook and chunk stoves. She became very good at splitting wood, even with the heavy splitting ax, and enjoyed it. Meantime, I did laundry and housecleaning—this being the only time of day I could give to these jobs—then did barn chores again and prepared supper. Afterwards, Nan did her homework, I read to Davis for a while and then put him to bed, then spent a short time in the living room reading or mending or hooking rug. I was just learning to hook rug and loved it. At nine o'clock or so I'd bed the house down for the night: bank the fires, let Dain and Annie out for a run, set the table for breakfast, let the animals back in—and then go to bed myself, not forgetting to wind the clock and set the alarm for 5:30.

Even going to bed wasn't final, because at least once during the night I'd have to get up to check my fires. They wouldn't last until morning without extra wood somewhere around two o'clock. Perhaps the realization, even in sleep, that to neglect my fires on a winter night would mean a real brisk kitchen in the morning served to waken me at the proper time, for I never had to set the clock for this event.

Nevertheless, it was pretty hard to leave a warm bed for the needed chore. Our bedroom is unheated except for a fire-place which we seldom use. The heat from the rest of the house keeps the temperature in there at least tempered, but that means anything from just above freezing to 45 degrees or so—seldom more. Hence I pay a good deal of attention to the bed and how I make it. Over the mattress I put a feather bed. Before the days of the electric blanket we used cotton-flannel sheets, a pair of heavy woolen blankets, and a thick quilt. In bed we wore cotton flannel nightgear, woolen bed socks, sometimes a scarf on the head, and took a pair of hot water bags along into the bargain. Under these circumstances bed was a cozy place, especially to get back into after a trip to tend the kitchen and living-room stoves.

Some of these winter nights were so beautiful that I couldn't resent the nightly chore. The bright moonlight shining on the snow up along the breast of the pasture, deer pawing the snow to get at the remains of the garden, and the still, tight cold that lay like a blanket on the land conveyed an impression that stays a long time in the files of the memory, to be taken out now and then and enjoyed all over again.

The normal daily routine at the farm was varied from time to time that winter when I went down to Mom's Place to spend the day with my youngest sister, who was now bedridden with rheumatoid arthritis. On occasions when Mom and Sid wanted to go off for the day I would load Davis and manuscript or proof, as the case was, into the car, go down to Mom's Place and spend the day with Betty.

Once while I was there it snowed all day—and how beautiful it was!—so that by the time Mom and Sid returned the roads were well covered. Without waiting to put chains on the Olds I started home, but on a hill the car lost its traction and I had to put chains on in snow so deep it filled my boots. On the last hill even the chains failed and the car slid backward into its favorite ditch, cuddling up against a steep rocky bank with only a thin cushion of snow between it and the rocks. I think it was at this point that my patience with the car finally gave out and that weekend when my husband was home we explored the possibility of turning the Olds in on a jeep. These versatile little vehicles were just coming on the civilian market and every farmer wanted one.

On weekends the usual weekday regime gave way to something a little different when both my husband and Mark were temporarily at home. Mark had to be fetched from the Aggie school; my husband usually caught a bus from Montpelier that dropped him off at the village store only a mile from home, and I'd meet him there. The procedure would have to be reversed, of course, on Sunday evening or early Monday morning.

The days the men folk spent at home were filled with chores such as adding to the wood supply in the shed for the hungry stoves—and what appetites they had on a cold winter day—checking on the animals, and attending to accumulated business in town. My husband did the barn chores on those days and in addition, when the time came, it was he who prepared the index for the new book, sitting at the kitchen table and spreading 3 x 5 slips all over it. It was a good index, too, and taught me a lesson on the advantages of nonperfectionism.

As another variation, I occasionally managed to get to Montpelier to spend part of the day listening to the sessions of the legislature. And once, when the Governor's Ball was to be held, my husband persuaded me to go up with him to attend it and spend the night. This meant all kinds of unusual and extraordinary arrangements at home, leaving Nan in charge and with my chores to do in addition to her own. Also she was not yet fifteen. Fortunately the ball was on a Friday evening and she didn't have to go to school the following day.

So when it was time to leave I packed my evening gear and headed north, not without some misgivings about sparks falling out of the chunk stove when a log was shoved into it, water pipes freezing in the cellar, and Davis falling downstairs. But I was determined to ignore my apprehensions and enjoy myself. In Montpelier, to change from heavy farm clothes and boots to a black velvet gown and scarlet slippers, all of which had unaccountably become a bit tight, was quite an experience. I felt a little like a butterfly coming out of its cocoon, or what I imagined that emergence into the world might feel like. To trail a long velvet skirt on the floor of a battered and borrowed jeep that was hardly more than a farm truck was another new sensation.

We had a marvelous lobster dinner at a local restaurant and then went across the street to the auditorium where the ball was to be held. Here the marble floor was hard on the feet, especially feet encased in tight slippers. I danced my share of dances, however, including a waltz with the Governor, and the gown created a pleasant impression. But the next morning I realized that I was only a farmer's wife after all, and instead of putting on my shoes I contented myself with sheepskin paks under galoshes and drove home fairly comfortably. Nan had done well with the fires and the water pipes, and she and the child were glad to see us.

As a student and teacher of government my husband found himself intensely interested in the organization, the politics, and the work of the General Assembly. When his turn came, he chose a seat somewhat at the back of the assembly chamber, was assigned to two committees, and then bided his time to speak while sizing up his colleagues.

He soon discovered that a Vermont Republican is more apt to hold to the beliefs of Jefferson than to those of the modern adherent to the Republican creed, and as he is first a Jeffersonian and secondly a Wilsonian, he found himself in friendly surroundings. Vermont is still a one-party state but that party is divided into a liberal and a conservative wing, and the liberal wing, which at that time included the Governor, often saw eye to eye with members of the Democratic party. The effect is a kind of informal two-party system that works pretty well in presenting both sides of important public issues.

My husband also discovered that the farmer members of the assembly keep their tongues still but their brains active: they say little during the debates but vote on the side of the angels. Having been elected largely by rural voters, he became a spokesman and sometimes even a strategist for the farmer representatives in the General Assembly as opposed to the lawyers and businessmen who generally speak more for urban interests.

Perhaps the outstanding experience of his service was his involvement in a move to create a public power authority, a state corporation to handle the electrical power to be made available through the development of the St. Lawrence Seaway. This was the public-private issue in the field of power, and then as now, it was a hot one. The bill had been drafted in the Governor's office; as my husband knows something about government corporations, he had had a hand in it and was asked to be one of its sponsors.

When the bill was finally introduced, a wrangle in committee and on the floor of the house followed in which no

holds were barred. Representatives of the private power interests came in droves to the capitol to present a show of force
and testify against the bill at committee hearings; the hearings
were so crowded with spectators that they had to be held in
the assembly chamber itself. Those who favored the power
authority bill were said to receive their orders direct from the
Kremlin, to be encouraging creeping socialism, and worse. The
proponents of the bill argued that it would assure cheap,
dependable power, but they made little impression and in the
end the measure was defeated. Such is the healing property
of time and the economic appeal of an ample supply of
power at a reasonable price, however, that in a later session
of the assembly a modification of the original plan was adopted
without controversy and put into effect in time to receive St.
Lawrence power when it became available. By that time also,
reference to the Kremlin was dropped and the red flag of
socialism furled and no longer used as a weapon by the private
power interests.

I had not realized that legislators could have as much fun
as these sometimes did. One day when I was in the gallery, for
example, a bill relating to the raising of frogs in the town of
Alburg to be sold to biology laboratories was offered in the
house and served as the launching pad for all kinds of facetious
arguments couched in the most formal kind of language and
uttered absolutely deadpan. One representative, the father of
nine children, solemnly got to his feet and said at some length
that for his part, he loved little animals. This was because of
a dear little fellow, a squirrel called Petie, who lived in a tree
in his backyard. Every morning, very early, Petie woke the
family with his cheerful little chatter under the window of the
master's bedroom. It was too early to get up, of course, and

too late to go back to sleep, and the result was . . . well, he did have nine children and in all gratitude he had to admit that he owed much of his good fortune to Petie. So of course he favored any bill that would protect the frogs of Alburg.

Incidents of this kind appeared spontaneously from time to time throughout the session and culminated in a mock session, held just before adjournment, which was a take-off on all the serious proceedings of the past months. I can remember a slim, elderly little lady-representative who took the part of a male colleague three times her weight and five times her girth. She borrowed a pair of his pants and stuffed them with pillows. And at a celebration dinner a few days later, she made a good deal of the fact that her husband had subsequently found the pants in her clothes closet.

*   *   *

While my husband was becoming increasingly involved in the work of the General Assembly, life at the farm went forward more or less as planned but with the occasional addition of something new to the compound. One of the best was the arrival of the new Universal Jeep to replace the used one we had borrowed from the agency after the Olds finally fell apart. A jeep is ugly to look at, uncomfortable to ride in, and lovely to drive.

This one was delivered to us in the middle of winter so there was ample time for it to prove itself on icy roads, in deep snow, and in mud. With the scars left by the Olds still fresh on our psyches, we watched the jeep's performance with a more than critical eye, but skepticism soon changed to utter devotion. Here was security on wheels, for which we were

134

glad to sacrifice soft cushions, resilient springs, roll-up windows, speed, and even silence.

To come up behind a line of stalled cars on an icy hill, slip into four-wheel drive and pass them all at a good clip was an exhilarating experience. To switch the gears to low ratio and then plow through mud so deep that it oozed through the holes in the drawbar made one master of a situation that formerly meant nothing but loss of time, temper, and energy. A jeep is the mechanical extension of the driver. Control is perfect. In low ratio the wheels never stop turning (although if there is no footing they may not go forward). We have travelled over fields, through woods, and on abandoned back roads where even a horse might have trouble. Once we had a little accident; the jeep skidded in a rut, went off the road, and landed on its side in a brook. It was hauled out with a wrecker, we added some oil to the crankcase, and drove home without more ado.

As it turned out, our only real trouble with that jeep was man-made—or rather, child-made. Davis was three that winter and of course was learning many new and exciting things in many places. One of his favorite places was the woodshed, and it was in the woodshed that we parked the jeep. One day when I called him in to lunch I found that he had managed to unscrew the cap of the gas tank and was busily shovelling dirt into it with a garden trowel.

This was serious. There is an expression come down to us from England, "beating the bounds," which originated in the fact that when a farmer, before the days of formal fences, wanted to convey to his son and heir the landmarks on the boundaries of his property, he took the boy for a walk and at each landmark, beat him so as to impress the spot on his memory. I think I had something like this in mind when I spanked Davis that day.

The spanking, however, was merely a precaution against future error and didn't undo the work of busy little hands that morning. I was due to fetch Mark in the afternoon from the Aggie school, and right after lunch I set out, dirty gas and all, with Davis on the seat beside me looking a little subdued. It is a tribute to the jeep that only on the way home did it begin to cough and stammer and then to stall. Each time we came to a forced stop Mark got out, unhitched the gas line from the carburetor, and sucked it clean. After about the third time his lips were white with the residue of gas but he made no complaint.

By the time we got home, Davis, who had watched these goings-on with wide eyes, was pretty well impressed all over again with the consequences of his morning's experiment. Fortunately, another advantage of a jeep is the simplicity of its design and construction, so Mark and I were able to detach the gas tank, empty it, and wash it out with gasoline. When I saw what was in it I was really impressed with the digestive system of a jeep because, in addition to large quantities of dirt, there was a stick of firewood some ten inches long, the jaw bone of a small animal (probably a lamb or a pig, but what was it doing in our shed? A good question) and a pile of small sticks and stones. Since neither Mark nor I had had much experience with this sort of job, we had some trouble getting the whole thing back together again but finally managed, and to Davis' credit let it be said that we never again had any more problems of this kind.

Another addition to the compound of our life that winter

was the arrival of Dain's first litter, which occurred rather inconveniently in the midst of the coldest weather. As in the case of Annie at the studio, we were alerted to the approach of Dain's confinement by her search for a nest. Being a large dog, this was not an easy quest to satisfy. I discouraged the use of the cellar because the dirt floor was cold and damp. So was the woodshed. Dain herself seemed to be mystified by the whole experience and kept looking at us with anxious eyes as though to say, "For Heaven's sake, what's happening to me?" If we left her alone for any length of time she was unhappy and afraid.

When her time finally came she chose the dark corner under Davis' crib in our bedroom. The first pup arrived early one evening and as others followed, Dain seemed more and more startled. But she tended to them as instinct told her, biting off the cords and licking each pup dry. By morning there were eight; before noon two more arrived.

All of which provided us with a bit of a problem. The pups couldn't remain under the crib nor could we put them outdoors. They would have to stay in the kitchen. So I built a pen under the kitchen table in the middle of the room and provided litter from torn newspapers—*The New York Times,* no less. Dain soon settled down and proceeded to take excellent care of her babies. But she still tried to keep an eye on Davis, too, and spent as much time as she could with him.

The pups grew like weeds, of course, and it was no time at all before they were able to climb out of the pen and roam all over the kitchen. Which presented yet another problem because, naturally, they weren't house-trained. But they were sweet and funny and cute, with wobbly legs and a sharp little bark when playing with one another, like baby animals the world over. As they were gradually weaned I fed them all together, grain and milk, out of a big pan. As they gathered enthusiastically around it, the over-all picture was one of ten earnest little rumps waggling with the effort of urging ten eager little heads to greater prowess in the pan.

Nevertheless, attached as we became to them, by the time they were six weeks old they were ready to go and we were ready to let them. So we advertised, and pretty soon I was able to dismantle the pen and give the floor the good scrubbing it needed. Dain had many litters after that but she no longer needed moral support and they were born in places more suitable to the occasion than the house. She came to favor the barn and so did we.

Then there was the adventure of the capons. Toward the end of the winter my husband got the idea that a good way for Mark to make some money during the coming summer would be to raise capons. Mark agreed, though not with any great show of enthusiasm that I could see, and for several weekends during the spring he and his father worked at cutting and setting poles and stringing chicken wire six feet high in a convenient spot on the upper place to make a proper run. Then they salvaged a couple of small henhouses, moved them into the run, and repaired them. They bought some feeding and watering equipment, provided litter for the houses, and in due course Mark installed two hundred young capons only a few weeks old, purchased from the Aggie school. Mark was still in school, however, and my husband still in Montpelier, so it fell to me to care for the capons during the week. No surprise to me, of course. Back in March I'd seen that part of it coming.

But there was more to it than merely feeding and watering.

The birds had only just been caponized by means of a simple operation in the back. In some cases this created a temporary opening between the chest cavity and the skin, allowing air to pass into the area between skin and body. Apparently it was a one-way passage because the air gradually collected under the skin until the bird began to look like a feathered balloon. The remedy was to puncture the skin and squeeze the air out. Up to a certain point, neither the accumulation of air nor its release seemed to be painful to the bird, but not to release the air would sooner or later result in death.

So twice a day I examined the flock to see if any bird was ballooning, then I'd catch it and with a pair of nail scissors, snip a little hole in the skin, squeeze the bird as one would a toy balloon, and hope that the puncture would stay open long enough to provide ventilation until the leak from the chest was healed. But generally the puncture closed again and on the next round, or even a second time on the same one, I'd have to snip and squeeze again. After experimenting with several different implements, I found that nail scissors were just right. It was impossible to sterilize them, of course, but there weren't any infections, either.

As anywhere from a dozen to two or three dozen birds had to be treated on each round, however, the job took quite a lot of my time, especially in the evening when it was already dusk and I had to use a flashlight. Once, after spending a day in Montpelier (Nan was visiting a friend and I had taken Davis with me), I got home pretty late and had to get fires started and Davis fed and settled for the night and other chores attended to before looking in on the capons. Many of them were badly swollen, so there was nothing for it but to go to work with the scissors (by that time I always carried them in my pocket) and it was after midnight before I got to bed.

After graduation at the Aggie school in June, Mark took full charge of his flock and it prospered well enough, but the final reckoning wasn't just what the entrepreneurs of the project had hoped for. After watching market prices for some time and scouting the local stores, Mark arranged for the disposal of the flock which by now numbered about 180 birds. So one morning family and flock were mobilized, we drove to a poultry-dressing plant, and there took part in an operation that started with sticking and ended with several crates of defeathered, market-dressed capons. But no one ever tried to discover whether the books showed a profit or a loss on the undertaking. I suspect, and I think the entrepreneurs did too, that if there was a profit to Mark, it was in about the same amount as the subsidy from his Dad.

* * *

Finally, there was the pig. As Emma's confinement approached in May it became clear that she could not be allowed to farrow in the dark little pen under the barn that had been her winter quarters. The government bulletin said she should have light and air. So one weekend when my husband was home we constructed a boxstall for her in what had once been the horse stable, and transferred her to it. This time we didn't need the bucket-over-the-head procedure; indeed, it would have been insulting. In addition to being heavy with little piglets, Emma was now a huge animal and walked very deliberately from one pen to the other. So nicely did she allow herself to be guided, in fact, that we considered changing her name to Angela.

Once in the boxstall, she seemed to appreciate the improvement in her quarters and settled down contentedly in the clean bedding. I doubt if there is any living creature that can look more contented than a pig, and my husband and I felt duly rewarded for our day of carpentering. Then he went back to Montpelier and I went back to studying the government bulletin.

A sow, it said, needs help when she farrows. It was not always so, of course, but it seems that civilization has affected pigs along with humans. You must note the signs of approaching confinement and make certain preparations. There must be a large tub, with clean rags and hot-water bottles in it, to receive the little pigs after they arrive and you have attended to them according to directions. The tub holds them until all are accounted for and the mother is able to give them her personal attention. If they are allowed to wander around the pen during farrowing, they are likely to be rolled on.

You must also have on hand, continued the bulletin, clean cloths to wipe the pigs with, clean cotton string to tie off the umbilical cord, a clean pair of sharp shears to cut the cord, a bottle of iodine into which to dip the end of the cord that remains on the pig, and a pair of clippers to snip off the sharp points of the four double teeth with which little pigs are born. The reason for this last operation is that if the points remain, the suckling piglet is apt to prick the sow, involuntarily she will jump a little, and might crush or maim a member of the litter.

So I made all the necessary preparations, rehearsed the procedure as well as I could without the presence of a little pig, and watched for signs of accouchement.

It was after supper one night when I went to the barn for

141

a final check on the situation that I found two little pigs running around in the pen, trailing their cords and seeming a little damp and bewildered, and Emma on her side apparently about to produce again. Davis was with me, it was nearly time for him to go to bed but obviously no time for me to put him there, Nan was away for the evening, my husband was in Montpelier, and the farm operator was milking the cows in the stable in another part of the big barn. So at the age of three, Davis had his first lesson in birth.

I told him to stand in the doorway of the boxstall so that Emma couldn't get out (she had no intention of trying, being otherwise fully occupied), while I caught the two pigs already born and popped them into the tub in time to catch the third as it made its appearance. I wiped it dry and then tried to tie off the cord, and right away learned the first lesson in pig-wifery: a little pig doesn't like to be turned on its back; if it is, it will squeal its head off, thus worrying the sow and causing her to try to get up in order to investigate, whereas her job requires her to lie on her side. So, as the bulletin might have said but didn't, it is necessary to hold the pig on its feet and tie off the cord mostly by feel. Even on its feet, when it is being held a little pig squirms like the bundle of muscle and nerve it is—it's amazing how strong and active a piglet can be at birth. Nevertheless, with patience the tying-off job can be done and improves with practice.

Clipping off the sharp little milk teeth is something else again, however, at least for one person to do alone because it means holding the squirming pig with one hand, holding its mouth open with a second, and using the clippers with a third. I finally gave up on that part of the job.

After the first two or three new arrivals I realized that

they were coming at a rate of something like one every fifteen minutes, so I took advantage of an interlude to get Davis back to the house, under protest, and to bed, then ran back to the barn in time to catch the next arrival. There were fourteen in all (a full tub) and the after-birth also appeared on schedule. When everything was taken care of I put the little pigs back into the pen while Emma lay quietly and gave them suck with a look of satisfaction-cum-exhaustion on her face—pigs do have such expressive faces! And quite a business the little pigs made of it, too.

Next morning when I went to the barn I found that one of them had been rolled on—a constant threat to a little pig—so I buried him under the rhubarb plant in the garden where he might still contribute to the farm economy.

I don't think there's anything cuter than a litter of little pigs, and for several days after that I spent hours in the barn watching them. They are so firm and hard, so pink and white and clean and active and playful, chasing each other around the pen and behaving a little like kittens and a little like puppies, but mostly like piglets. I don't wonder that the pig is my husband's favorite domestic animal.

When I finally got back to the house the night of the farrowing, the phone was ringing and it was my husband from Montpelier calling as he sometimes did just to hear how things were going. He had been ringing at intervals for several hours this time and was worried that some catastrophe had wiped out the entire family. When I reported on Emma he laughed in relief and later told his colleagues about it, with the result that when next I visited Montpelier someone asked me about my evening in the barn and I had to give a blow-by-blow account.

Emma remained with us for several years, producing two litters a year but always, after that first one, refusing assistance and getting along very well without it. But she also got bigger and heavier. Being Yorkshire, she had great length and although normally this breed does not have very much fat, with the years it did begin to come on her. Her size and weight were finally such that she could not avoid accidentally crushing her offspring. She would lie down ever so gently and slowly, one leg at a time, with infinite caution, but the final letting go was often sudden and there would be a death in the family. So the time came when we were forced to decide that Emma had had her day. She was our friend but we were farmers, and farming is based on the facts of life, including death as well as birth. So one day on the table in my pantry I was presented with a great deal of pork to prepare for the freezer, hams and bacon to cure, and lard to render down. The hams alone weighed 45 pounds apiece after trimming, and the sides of bacon were a yard long.

Toward the end of May my husband came back from his service in the General Assembly somewhat battle-scarred but not seriously hurt. The worst of it had been the fight over the public power authority bill on which he had been defeated and in the course of which he had been called everything from a socialist to a sap. Such calumnies bothered him but not enough to prevent him from accepting an invitation to speak on the public power issue in a series of debates with the head of one of the private power companies, scheduled to be held throughout the state in the following fall.

Meanwhile there was the summer to think about and this one would not be on the farm. My husband had been offered a visiting professorship in the summer session of New York

University and since the family exchequer was heading for a lean period he decided to accept. As for me, I really didn't care too much what happened for a while so long as I didn't have to do anything about it. I was just plain bone-tired.

CHAPTER 10

Freedom to Travel

OUR EXPERIMENT IN FREEDOM FROM THE INSTITUTION WAS working out on the farm pretty much as we expected it would and in some ways—especially financially—it was lots better. There had been no lean period that we couldn't cope with. Now we discovered that we were free not only to live our own kind of life in a locality of our own choosing; we were free also to travel when the opportunity presented itself. This aspect of freedom developed spontaneously out of the need to replenish the family exchequer as increasing costs for education were anticipated.

The summer at New York University was the first absence from the farm and it turned out to be the forerunner of several, all of which were interesting and profitable, and proved, if proof were needed, that we owned the farm and were not owned by it. When an invitation was received to teach for a semester and my husband accepted it, I packed what was needed, we made a few arrangements at home, and departed without more ado. The farm operator was not a hired man but a partner in the enterprise and worked largely on his own responsibility, with general oversight by my husband in matters of land- and herd-management. Since he was willing to look after our personal animals during our absences, it was easy for us to go off for several months at time, and on at least one occasion, for more than a year.

So easy was it, indeed, that for more than a decade we didn't even lock the door when we left. There is no key to the front door anyhow; it closes with a bolt but the house settled and the bolt doesn't work. There is a key to the back door but it hangs unused on a hook in the kitchen. As a precaution, however, I did put a hook on the outside of the back door high enough so that Dain couldn't reach it and let herself in, and then leave the door open when she departed. To close a door was something she never could be bothered with. It is true, of course, that without the presence of the farm operator and his family in the cottage across the road, we couldn't have been so casual in the matter of locks. As it was, we never lost anything.

That summer in New York was easily arranged. My husband's sister and his aunt had planned to come east, and they cheerfully agreed to take over the management of the farm household, including the three children, during our absence. A friend in the city found a sublease for us in a cool little flat in Greenwich Village, with a porch and an ivy-covered garden attached to it. After a two-year respite, my husband returned to teaching with a sense of exhilaration that was a pleasure to live with. Once before, during World War II, he had commuted from Washington to teach one night a week at New York University and had found the students stimulating and responsive. Those in the summer session proved to be the same.

As for me, I had nothing to do and nearly fell flat on my face. Another girl and I had once taken a walking trip in the Black Forest, carrying our gear in knapsacks that became quite heavy if we packed very much food. One day after a long climb followed by a rather steep descent of a mile or more on a forest path, we stopped at an inn for a picnic lunch in its hospitable garden. As I slung my knapsack off my back, my bodily center of gravity suddenly shifted and there was a sensation of nearly falling on my face. In a figurative sense, I had the same sensation when we settled into the New York flat.

Instead of falling forward, however, I fell back into an armchair and put my feet up. I spent most days sitting quietly at home, reading (fiction or whodunits), sewing a little, napping a lot, and occasionally studying the habits of the cats that made more or less regular rounds through the back yards and gardens of West Eleventh Street. Indeed, I doubt if my brain could have coped with a subject of any higher intellectual content. It was in a state of mental and physical inertia that made me resent even a phone call before late afternoon.

After that, however, I was ready for the social activities of the evening, whatever they might be, and often they were very pleasant. New York in summer is one of the nicest places in the world. Many people leave it and those who remain adopt an attitude of informality and relaxation that is wholly agreeable. We enjoyed this aspect of the city and found that, like ourselves—and probably for the same reasons—many of our friends also remained in town instead of migrating to the country during the hot season.

*   *   *

A second absence from the farm a few months after our return from New York, was to accept a visiting professorship at Occidental College near Los Angeles for the second semester of the academic year. This would mean closing the house in the middle of winter, which, however, was no great task since our plumbing was still primitive and there was no hot-water system at all. Mark had graduated from the Aggie school and was now enrolled at the University of Vermont. My husband, Nan, and Davis would fly to the coast to the home of my husband's parents in San Bernardino, near Los Angeles. We would make our headquarters with them, my husband would commute to LA for classes twice a week, and Nan would attend the local high school. We exchanged the jeep for a jeep station wagon which I would drive to California with most of our luggage plus the files and books from which we seem never to be parted.

Everything would have gone according to plan except that as I was fixing my hair one cold morning in January, a week before departure, I noticed that the area under my left ear was swollen. Also it was sore to the touch. There was mumps in the neighborhood and apparently it was my turn. I exclaimed my dismay to my husband who was still in bed. The consequences of such an illness just at this time might be serious because neither of the children had had it, they might be quarantined, plane tickets were already bought, and the date for the opening of the semester in California was immovable.

I finished dressing quickly, abandoned the family and drove down to Mom's Place before breakfast. She and Sid took me in, offered sympathy, comfort, and repose while the rest of the family carried on at the farm. During the next few days

I rested and read Balzac. My husband and Nan closed the house at the farm, turned Dain over to the farm operator's family, and then, with Davis, came down to Mom's Place to say goodbye. I waved to them from the dining-room window and they departed. I went back to the couch and my book before the open fire and pretty soon Mom served tea and it was very pleasant indeed.

But not everyone was happy. This was Dain's first separation from her family and it proved to be the last. She had always shown affection for the four children in the cottage but her first allegiance was to Davis. When he left, she mourned him, if not the rest of us. On the night after the family's departure and our house was empty, I was wakened at Mom's Place by the wailing of a sorrowful dog, bereft and desolate. I caught a glimpse of her standing in the snow in the moonlight in an open barway behind Mom's house, crying her misery, and no more sorrowful sound had I ever heard. I went to call her and comfort her but by the time I got to the door she was gone.

After that she quickly settled in with the farmer's family, all of whom loved her dearly. She became one of them, full of responsibility for their comings and goings, and took their little girl to fill the place of Davis in her heart. Thereafter she was always glad to see us when we returned to the farm and was invariably courteous and considerate in her behavior toward us. But her allegiance was now to the other family and we judged it better for her to leave it that way. In the cottage she became one of the children, and yet a little above them, too. So close was she to them that when the littlest girl was telling us one Sunday that her mother had taken them to church she noted that the family group had not been complete.

"Daddy and Dain," she explained, "aren't Catholics, so they didn't come in."

Years later when Dain had to be put to sleep, the effect in the cottage was as though one of the children had died.

*　　*　　*

Two weeks after my family departed for California I had recovered enough to follow them. I packed the car, took ten days for a leisurely trip across the country alone (my favorite method of travel—no one argues with me if I want to stop or don't want to), and arrived in San Bernardino in time to enjoy the balmy winter season, a warm greeting from my family, and a beautiful red felt knitting bag as a valentine from my husband.

In the next few months, the second semester of the academic year, my husband enjoyed his teaching and also a number of speaking engagements at several of the colleges in the area. It was fun living with the family, we made and remade some friendships in both the town and gown categories, and went on two camping trips, one a packtrip into the High Sierras to fish for golden trout. Nan settled into the local high school without difficulty and Davis had chicken pox. There was no pressure on my time and I was free to accompany my husband on most of his comings and goings. He received another offer of a summer-session appointment, this time to conduct at the University of Michigan a seminar in the social and political aspects of atomic energy. He accepted, so, instead of returning directly to the farm when we left California, we spent six weeks at Ann Arbor.

Getting there was on a less casual basis than that on which

the trip to the coast had been, however, because now I had Davis with me (my husband had gone ahead by plane to make a detour by way of Washington), and the child's opinion of the trip was illustrated in the fact that when he pretended to prepare a meal for me in the backseat of the car, it consisted entirely of "soup ice cream," two foods he detested. An unhappy climax to the drive occurred on the downgrade into Denver. Davis had been tired and I had finally managed to get him to sleep on the backseat. On a piece of rough road that was under construction, I looked back just in time to see a flower pot containing a small cactus plant topple off its perch above the backseat. I grabbed for it but it eluded me and spilled a mass of dry dirt onto Davis' upturned face. The immediate crisis was compounded of shock to the child, dirt in his eyes and mouth, only a thermos of water with which to cope with the situation, and the car pulled off onto a rough shoulder to allow traffic to pass among the bulldozers and graders and trucks.

Once recovered from the shock, however, Davis was a good sport about the whole thing and his serenity was mostly restored by the time we pulled into Denver for the night. The following morning while high-tailing through Nebraska I slowed down to about 45 miles an hour, pulled over to the side of the road, and watched Davis as he took the offending cactus in its pot and dropped it out the window.

The summer at Ann Arbor passed very pleasantly. My husband enjoyed his teaching; atomic energy was still a novelty, and his course was an attempt at breaking new ground. In our neighborhood, Davis had an initial encounter with the cannibalistic characteristics of the in-group (he was the only outsider), but reacted with his usual energy and by the end of our stay was on good terms with the cannibals. I was occupied with the final stages of production on a textbook—proof and index—which I accomplished, mainly on coffee, in a cool little basement study.

At the end of the summer we drove back to Vermont and realized all over again how much we loved the farm. How green everything seemed after the withered browns of southern California and the sparse summer tones of Michigan! The place was in good shape and we settled in for the fall with deep pleasure, especially as the autumn colors that year were magnificent.

Mark, meanwhile, had transferred from the University of Vermont to Pomona College in California. It was his Dad's alma mater, but being a wholly private institution, it was more expensive than UVM. Considering the probability that we would be traveling a good deal, it had seemed best for Nan to remain in California with her grandparents, finish high school, and then go on to Pomona too, this being her choice as well as Mark's. The prospect of several years of college expenses moved my husband to accept an invitation that fall to teach during the second semester as a visiting professor at the University of Puerto Rico and we looked forward not only to fattening the exchequer but to spending a pleasant winter in a warm climate as well.

It meant leaving the farm in the middle of winter again, but this time there were no obstacles such as mumps. We packed a few belongings, took the train to New York, shed our heavy coats, scarfs, gloves, and boots into the arms of accommodating friends at the airport, and ran through the icy wind to where the plane was parked on the apron. The following morning the Puerto Rican steward pointed to his

153

homeland on the horizon and extolled the beauty of "the green snows of Puerto Rico" in a voice that betrayed his dislike of the white snows of the mainland.

We spent a delightful four months in Rio Piedras, the site of the university, living in a furnished flat that was new and easy to care for. After we had grown used to the tempo of life on the Island—it is slow and to become impatient is to irritate oneself needlessly and wholly without effect—we relaxed the way the Islanders do and got to know something of the people, their history, their customs, and their cooking.

We enrolled Davis in a nearby kindergarten where he became the object of the affections of a little girl in red shoes and brilliant earrings, who once announced to my husband when he went to fetch Davis, "He ees my mahn!" For my part, a difficulty I encountered right away was how to fill my time. I had been working at close to top speed for several months, and now, suddenly, everything was minimal. Again I had the "knapsack feeling," the staggering imbalance that follows the sudden shifting of the body's center of gravity. To restore the balance, sewing and reading weren't enough so I studied Spanish. I bought a grammar, a dictionary, and then a series of paperback novels in Spanish (which, however, I found to be mostly translations from the French). At the end of four months I had a good grounding in grammar and could read fiction with only an occasional reference to the dictionary. But I never could speak the language nor understand what was said to me in it.

One of the main enjoyments in Puerto Rico is the food. Dishes made with chicken and rice in a number of variations are wonderful. Suckling pig, roasted whole until the rind is crisp and the meat succulent, is a specialty. Shrimp and rice, and squid or baby octopus and rice (served in "ink" because the juice of the squid is black) are delicious. The native beef, however, is to be avoided. Most of it, I think, comes from superannuated oxen retired from the sugarcane fields, and it is no accident that the only recipe for beef in my Puerto Rican cookbook is called "Old Clothes" because after the long cooking required, that is what the product finally looks like.

Then there are all kinds of wonderfully delicious native fruits and vegetables. A farmers' market in a covered arcade offers great quantities of produce of every native variety and fascinating aspect, in addition to the varieties with which Americans are more familiar. Of some fruits, especially pineapple and papaya, we never seemed to get too much. I experimented with all sorts of native dishes, with varying degrees of success and much pleasure.

A special delight in Puerto Rico was the French bread, the formula for which dates back to a certain French chef who accompanied his refugee employers from New Orleans to the Island at the time of the Louisiana Purchase. This loaf is long and crusty and delicious, especially when you fetch it direct from the bakery, still warm from the oven. On such occasions it is the mainstay of a wonderful lunch, with fresh butter, a green salad, a piece of cheese, and papaya to finish off. Finally, the liquor in Puerto Rico is plentiful and cheap so long as one confines oneself to rum, which we did. Rum is a good hot-climate drink and can be served in many interesting combinations.

The swimming in Puerto Rico is marvelous. There are many beaches; a certain one called Luquillo is a large crescent of white sand, bordered with palm trees and lapped by the blue

Atlantic, its leisurely rollers breaking, on a fine day, in a long lazy line of white foam that creeps up the gentle incline of the beach and then retreats, only to try again when the next roller comes in. Among the palms are individual bath houses, picnic tables, and benches. Every now and then we'd go there with a basket packed with steak, fresh French bread, fresh butter, green onions, fruit, and a bottle of red wine. After a swim and a bask in the sun for a while, we'd gather fuel— drift wood, palm fronds, coconut shells—and make a fire in an enclosure of stones. Then we would broil the steak, eat chunks of fresh bread and butter with green onions laid on, sip the wine, and finish off with fruit, after which we'd nap in the shade, swim, read, or just do nothing. It was always a satisfactory outing.

A most delightful experience, Puerto Rico; a leisurely, renewing experience, what the French call "reculer pour mieux sauter," or "retreat a little in order to jump the better." Perhaps our pleasure on the Island was summed up in a remark by Davis. We asked him one day which he liked better, Vermont or Puerto Rico. When he chose Puerto Rico, we asked him why.

"Because," he said, "you don't have to wear almost not nothing."

It was also in Puerto Rico that we got a further insight into Davis' character, especially his independence. Among the Islanders, baby-sitting is regarded as a menial occupation and hence the girls at the university on whom one would ordinarily rely, are not available. Most local families include at least one elderly member who is willing to keep an eye on the children, but of course we lacked that advantage. Shortly after we were settled, we were invited out for an evening. We waited until Davis was asleep—he sleeps soundly and rarely wakes in the night. We had no fear of fire because the house was built of poured concrete and there were no drapes or hangings. Also our landlord occupied the flat above and we told him we would be gone for a couple of hours.

But naturally we worried should Davis perhaps wake to find himself alone. So the second time that we went out after he was asleep, we told him about it the following morning. He was interested in where we had been, and with whom, and what we'd had to eat, but he showed no concern at all for himself. A few days later there was another invitation and this time we told him of it in advance.

"Do you think you'll be all right?" I asked him.

"Oh yes," he said. "Just leave the light on in the hall in case I have to go to the bathroom."

So thereafter that was our normal procedure and it worked very well. Davis has always felt secure so long as the light is out in his room and the door is closed. For him, darkness has a warm cozy quality that he loves.

*   *   *

Puerto Rico was fun but we were glad to get back to Vermont in late May in time to take off the storm windows and put in the garden. Our period of leisure came to an abrupt end when we resumed farm work and housework and, in addition, my husband started to write another textbook. The subject of this one was public administration and I was to be associated with him as co-author. We had to get a good start on it that summer because in September we were to go to Tallahassee for the first semester at Florida State University. This would mean combining writing with teaching, which is not ideal but we'd done it before while still in Evanston and figured we could do it again.

Also by now Davis was five years old, bored with kindergarten and ready for first grade. His sixth birthday was not until the following February, however, so he wasn't legally eligible for public school in Vermont, or, as we discovered, in Florida either. But we also learned that if he were presented to the Florida public-school system as a transfer from another public school they would be obliged to accept him. We put the matter to the principal of the school in Bethel and, being a philosopher rather than a bureaucrat, he saw our point and enrolled Davis in first grade. So I bought the child a new pair of shoes, a red hunting cap, and a lunch box, and for a week he went off to school each morning with the other children from Christian Hill, running to take his place in the neighbor's station wagon that doubled as school bus. At the end of the week the principal gave me a transfer card with the comment,

"There, that should get him into Heaven itself."

The next day we packed the jeep wagon with a pair of typewriters, several cartons of files, a briefcase of manuscript, a few clothes (I didn't even take a hat); then we closed the kitchen door, hooked it against Dain, said goodbye to our friends in the cottage, and headed south. It was mid-September.

In Tallahassee we sublet a pleasant furnished house from an absent professor, turned the guest room into a study for my husband and the dinette into a study for me (there was also a dining room), enrolled Davis in a fine new public school only two blocks away, and settled down to a routine of teaching-cum-writing that worked well.

Again, in our leisure moments, we explored the country and the local mores, made friends, and became familiar with local cooking. Grits, corn bread, spoon bread, fish, chick-peas, and greens cooked with a little fat pork became staples in the pattern of our diet. And we learned, too, that southern hospitality is no myth.

One mishap in Tallahassee might have been serious. On a Saturday morning that Davis was home, I was typing in the dinette while he tried to amuse himself on the front lawn. A house in an urban residential quarter is not like a house in the country and Davis missed his woodshed. Suddenly I heard a scream with an urgency in it that I had never heard before. After about five hours (or so it seemed to me) I was out through the kitchen and down off the back porch and Davis was staggering toward me. I caught him as he fell and when I got his shoe off, his foot was already deep purple, the result of a haematoma, and swelling even as I looked at it. He had tried to climb into a concrete birdbath, but the top, which weighed some seventy-five pounds, wasn't hitched to the base and had fallen on his foot.

We got him to the hospital, which wasn't far away. X-ray determined that no bone was broken, fortunately, and a cast kept the foot at rest while it healed. After a couple of days in bed with an ice pack on the cast, Davis went back to school on crutches—and became very good at handling them too. Being largely immobilized, he spent his afternoons sitting in a big armchair in the living room listening to radio. This occupation soon made him an expert on soap opera, and the immobility added five pounds to a frame that had always been a little on the spare side. After a couple of weeks he remarked that his foot felt "just like a foot again" and when the cast was removed there seemed to be no evidence there was going to be any permanent ill effect from the accident.

The experience of Christmas in Florida was a rather odd one for northerners but we enjoyed it well enough. We enjoyed especially the masses of camellias that begin blooming everywhere in that part of the state in the early winter. In January we completed the manuscript of the textbook (written once by my husband and edited and retyped twice by me) and sent it off to the publisher. My husband gave and graded his final exams, we packed, closed the house, and headed north.

By the time we reached New York it was snowing, and thereafter with each hundred miles we added clothing to ourselves and antifreeze to the radiator of the jeep wagon. On the farm the hardest part of the winter still lay ahead. But pleasant as the south had been, we welcomed the snow. Piled in deep drifts around the house, it served as insulation and made the house warm and snug within. There was a shed full of firewood and a freezer full of food. Davis rejoined the first grade at the local school and did well. My husband happily changed gears from professor and author to farmer, and I shifted from faculty wife to farmer's wife with equal pleasure.

Then things began to happen, and that spring is still known to us as "the spring my husband was away." First, he accepted an invitation to spend a week in Puerto Rico for a series of lectures, then another to go almost immediately afterward to England for conferences and more lectures. He would be gone for more than a month. Most of his absence would occur in March and April, which is usually mud season and also sugaring season in our part of Vermont. Our jeep wagon was not of the four-wheel drive variety and would be virtually useless when the roads were bad, but the farm operator drove a regular jeep and would be able to get his children and Davis to and from school.

The experience that followed my husband's departure was one which I had not anticipated but which I recognized at once as something special, and I settled down to savor every moment of it. Let no one suppose that I do not love my husband, for I do. Also I missed him. Nevertheless, it came to me as a delightful shock to realize that another form of freedom is freedom for privacy.

Once Davis was off to school in the morning, I had the whole day to myself. He returned in mid-afternoon and spent the remaining hours of daylight playing with the children from the cottage, sliding on hillsides where snow remained, playing in the barn, or just messing about in the woodshed. The weather at first was sugaring weather, warm sunny days and cold, often freezing, nights. From time to time there was a light snowfall called a sugar snow. As the season progressed, buds appeared on the maples, putting an end to sugaring, the ground became bare, the birds began to reappear after their winter in the south, the deer emerged from winter quarters to feed on dried grass on sunny southern slopes; and underfoot it was very, very soft and wet.

In the house I got down to a round of daily occupations that delighted me. The manuscript of the textbook we had completed in Florida came back from the publisher with suggestions for several changes; I took care of these in the bright, sunny study upstairs. Then I caught up on a number of jobs that had been neglected during our absences: the filing of correspondence and newspaper clippings and reprints and reports—that mass of paper that flutters about a professor's home like a snowstorm. I also classified and filed a pile of clippings having to do with the various aspects of farming: animal care, land management, soil conservation, house plants, and the like. Also recipes that I had collected from various sources and had never had handy to try; now I filed them all and tried some of them. I also went back to my hooked rug and made good progress on it.

And then I read books I had "always wanted to read but had never got around to." Among others, there were the exciting books of Mary Parker Follett, a spinster lady from Boston whom I met many years before when she visited Geneva and I acted as her guide around the Secretariat of the League of Nations. I had read her book called *Creative Experience* while we were living in Evanston. Now I proceeded to read *The New State*, and a collection of her lectures and essays entitled *Dynamic Administration*. The wisdom, the understanding, the objectivity, the insights into human personality and motivation I gleaned from these books during those spring evenings before the living room fire was an experience for me that is unforgettable. It enhanced the quality of everything I did during those days, made me jealous of time spent off the place, led me to decline invitations from friends in town on the score that the roads were so bad I couldn't travel them, although in fact I could have done so had it been necessary.

There is much talk these days about "togetherness." I revelled in "aloneness," and was almost bad-tempered at the thought of it coming to an end as I drove one afternoon to White River Junction to meet my husband, returning from his long absence. The reunion cured my temper all right, but the memory of freedom for privacy remains with me.

*   *   *

Right after that I also had an unexpected chance to travel. For some time, Mom had been going to Switzerland for the winter, since it was hard for her to live on her own place in the cold weather and Sid wasn't always available to look after her and drive the car. This spring, while still in Switzerland, Mom had a thrombosis which blinded her left eye. As an experienced traveller she could have made the journey home alone all right but I was worried and in the end decided to fetch her back myself.

On short notice, therefore, I got a passport and plane passage and set out just as I was coming down with pinkeye. One of the horses on the farm had had it, then the farmer's children, and when Davis came down with a mild case, I put a pair of dark glasses in the handbag I would take on my trip. It was a wise precaution; this ailment causes an adult female to look like a hag of a hundred and ten, and any disguise is welcome. As an additional bother, my suitcase was misplaced on a change of planes in Paris but that turned out all right: I had a chance to learn at first hand that most people travel with too much luggage. Once arrived in Vevey I borrowed a nightgown and a blouse from Mom and got along very well for the five days that elapsed before the suitcase turned up.

To return to Switzerland after an absence of thirty years, to the same small town in which I had spent four years as an adolescent and where I still had friends dating from my school days there, was another experience that was unanticipated and likewise unforgettable. Mom and I stayed on for a week after I arrived, to give me a chance to recover from the pinkeye, renew my youth, and pack Mom's trunk and suitcases—she always travelled commodiously so far as luggage was concerned.

At first it was like walking around in a dream peopled by vivid ghosts of the past, but gradually the activities of the moment gained dominance and became real. I spent a day on a favorite mountain, taking the little cog railway up and walking down. Judging by the way my knees felt for the next few days, it might have been better had I walked up and ridden down. But acres and acres of wild narcissus were in bloom on the slopes of that particular mountain, a specialty of that time and place that makes it look like snow fields in May, so creaky knees really didn't matter. I revisited houses in which we had once lived and recognized familiar faces in the stores and among the tradespeople.

Switzerland changes as all places do, but less than most except to get better ordered, cleaner (if that is possible), more prosperous looking, greener below the snowline, brighter with flowers, and better cared for. Maybe this is why most people agree that La Suisse is a very solid and beautiful nation, but seldom get much beyond that judgment. It is less often realized that the Swiss also uphold the freedom of the individual to be his own idiosyncratic self, if that is his desire. If a person observes certain amenities that have to do mostly with the comforts and rights of others in the community—like waiting for passengers to descend from the bus before boarding, like crossing the street at places marked for that purpose (your insurance becomes invalid if you are struck by a car while crossing at an unmarked spot), like saying "Good morning" to the sales clerk on entering a shop and

"Thank you" and "Goodbye" on leaving it—if a person observes these little amenities, then he can dress, speak, and believe as he likes and no one will think it unusual or will criticize him for it. For centuries all kinds of rebels and dissidents have taken refuge in Switzerland and all have been tolerated if not actually welcomed, regardless of their beliefs, whether good, bad, or just silly.

Mom and I came home on the *Queen Mary*. When we arrived in Vermont the lilacs were in bloom. I left Mom with Sid in Hanover, cleaned up her house, laid a fire in the living-room fireplace, filled vases with lilacs and the last of the apple blossoms, and then, with two good friends, fetched her home one afternoon in time to prepare tea and watch her pour it for her guests from her usual high-backed chair beside the fireplace, with much charm and good humor—a little in the regal manner of the grande dame which, in fact, she was.

CHAPTER 11

Christian Hill Barbecue

THAT SUMMER SAW THE END OF WHAT NEARLY BECAME A permanent annual event in our community, one for which my husband and I were partly responsible and in which we became deeply involved.

In many rural neighborhoods there is at least one person who serves as a kind of spark plug, and in ours this was the wife of a close neighbor. Abbie is a slender, energetic, dynamic, hard-working woman of the sort who prefers to be outdoors rather than indoors, and there was an instant affinity between us when we met for the first time. It was she who looked after me from her house on the hill above us during three months that I spent alone on the farm one year during the war. It was she who, on a cold winter evening, would come down the hill belly-flop on the barn sled under the pretext of using our phone but really to check on me, my morale, and my wood pile.

Abbie always knows where the first fern brakes are to be found in the spring and taught me to identify those that are edible; cooked like asparagus, fern brake tastes like asparagus.

166

Abbie taught me about milkweed greens and wild horseradish cooked together, a delicious combination said to thin the blood and overcome its winter sluggishness. She makes the best elderberry jam in five counties. She knows where the wild strawberries and wild raspberries grow best and although she never quite introduced me personally to her private berrying grounds, I found some of them for myself after she left the neighborhood.

Abbie loves a neighborhood party and almost any excuse will serve. A housewarming is a fine one, but in a fairly stable community such as Christian Hill, the opportunity doesn't often arise. When we bought our place in the summer of 1940 she welcomed the event and organized a housewarming, but things moved a little too fast on that occasion, the house burned before it could be suitably warmed, and the party had to be called off.

If no other reason for a gathering presented itself, Abbie was always ready with a little book in which she kept a record of the birthdays and wedding anniversaries of everyone in the vicinity. Several of these fell in June—six or seven of them—and it was an annual event with her to convene a party in celebration thereof. When we built the pond beyond our garden, there was a natural picnic spot beside it and it soon became the locale for such affairs. Abbie would make the rounds of the neighborhood (there was no question of a selective guest-list because everyone was invited), and on the day itself each family brought a cake or cookies or sandwiches and Abbie made up a freezer—or maybe two freezers—of ice cream. If it could be obtained that early in the season, there would also be watermelon, chilled in the cooler in our milk house. I supplied the coffee. I also rounded up as many garden

167

chairs as I could for the benefit of the elderly, but most of us sat on the ground.

Of course no one could attend such a gathering until after evening chores, so no one showed up until seven or later. The food was spread on an improvised table—our cellar door laid on sawhorses with a sheet for a cloth did very well—and the guests helped themselves. Then Abbie served the ice cream direct from the freezer (the dasher would already have been removed and some child would have had the exquisite pleasure of licking it), and I brought coffee from the house where I brewed it in a big canner on the stove.

Then we'd sit around and gossip—with the men usually off in a group by themselves—and maybe listen to records on a portable player. As the dew began to fall I'd fetch jackets and rugs for those whose bones felt the dampness. And finally around ten o'clock or so we'd all renew our good wishes and congratulations to those who had been honored, say good night, and the party would be over.

It was at one of these June gatherings before taking up permanent residence that I inadvertently became co-progenitor of the Christian Hill barbecue. It happened at a time when I was concentrating on several new kinds of work. I was attempting to prepare an index for a textbook and instead of taking a few days to it I was spending almost a month. Davis was only six months old and I was pretty much occupied with him, too. Then there was the usual housework to carry on and no labor-saving devices (which, as a matter of fact, probably saved me a good deal of labor in work that never got done at all). The June picnic was well under way and I was feeling relaxed and a little slaphappy—surely not a state in which to make a rational decision on anything, much less a complicated community performance.

At this point a neighbor remarked that he thought it would be a good idea to have a barbecue. Without even thinking, I agreed. He had been reading an article about a barbecue held in Texas with a whole animal cut up into roasts and cooked in a pit. We talked in the group about the idea at some length and even planned a menu and the kind and breed of animal that would be suitable for the pit.

The next day I went back to my index and my baby and forgot all about barbecues until a week or so later when the neighbor came to see me. We should call a meeting, he said, get a committee organized, pick a date for the barbecue. He kept after me and others on the hill until finally we did call a meeting and then settled the matter of the committee by simply putting everyone there on it—even those who came chiefly for the sociability and the refreshments were caught in the net.

My husband and another neighbor who was a kind of jack-of-all-trades were made co-chairmen but I was right when I suspected from the start that it was I who would do most of the work. We chose a date for the latter part of August when the weather was supposed to be generally favorable, and picked a site in a pasture beside a brook where there was the added advantage of a pile of old lumber that might be used to build serving tables. We appointed a treasurer and settled the price of the meal (one dollar) without knowing anything about probable costs, including the price of the beef. We found someone to take care of the printing and distribution of tickets. But how many tickets—one hundred, three hundred?

No idea. Where would we find a beef animal? No idea. And who would cook it? Same answer.

The whole proposition was a mass of formlessness. There would be a good deal of running around to bring some kind of order into it, and we had no car, having sold ours early in the war. The young man who worked our place did have one, or at least what passed for a car, a faded old light-blue Dodge sedan. A tree had fallen on it, bashing in the roof over the driver's seat and causing it to leak in wet weather. And in the preceding mud season its radiator had exploded during a heroic effort to get up the hill to our place, making a large hole somewhat below the water line that had never been repaired. By regular refilling, however, the radiator could be made to serve. What was left of the car was sturdy and had character; we were glad to borrow it.

The first thing was to find the beef and the cook. Meat rationing was still in force and there was a lively demand for beef on the hoof. Inquiries turned up a man called Riley Bostwick who lived in a nearby town and raised Angus beef cattle and who in addition had been an army cook in World War I. It sounded like an ideal combination. Taking the old car, I called on him and found him working in the barnyard of his mountain farm. I on one side of the fence, he on the other, I introduced myself and stated my errand. He folded his arms on the top rail, bowed his head, and gazed at the ground in a most unencouraging manner. He didn't say a word, just listened as I kept on talking. Then he remarked in a mild sort of way that he had a long waiting list for his beef.

The whole enterprise seemed like a bootless one and in a final, rather desperate effort at persuasion I said that, well, this was not a benefit or something to raise money for anything.

"It's just a bunch of neighbors who want to get together for a community affair," I added. "A gathering of local people who want to have a good meal together."

Mr. Bostwick raised his head quickly and gave me a sharp look from his pale and penetrating blue eyes.

"Community affair, eh?" he said. "Well, let's see what I've got."

With that he escorted me to a pasture where a half-dozen yearling heifers and steers were grazing and invited me to take my pick. By this time he had told me something of his own interest in community activities, local civic spirit, and local responsibility for the conduct of local affairs, and I began to understand his sudden change of attitude. I chose a nice fat young heifer, he seemed to approve, we made an agreement as to price (he shaved it from what he asked his private customers), and set the day on which we would fetch it from the local freezer-locker where he would have it hanging for ten days or so before the barbecue.

When I began to talk about a cook, however, he said he couldn't do the job himself, he'd been away from it too long. On that we parted, but thus began a friendship that endures.

It started to rain that week and was pouring pitchforks the day I set out with Nan and a neighbor's daughter to find a cook. The trail led to a barn that a former barbecue cook was helping to build in a nearby town. I told him my story and asked if he would do the job.

"Well," he said, "to barbecue a beef requires special equipment. Or anyhow, it does the way we do it."

There had to be a roasting pan, he said, large enough to

take the whole animal. This pan had to be set on cleats inside a larger pan designed to hold a couple of inches of water. Then there had to be a hood to cover the whole rig, which in turn stands on an arch, as the term is. An arch is a kind of furnace built on the ground, some two feet high and as long and wide as the pan that is set on it. An arch made of concrete is commonly used in boiling maple sap to make syrup. In the barbecue pasture it would be made of stones and chinked with sods. When the fire is kindled in the arch, the water boils in the bottom pan, steam gathers beneath the hood, and the meat is cooked whole, slowly, and all the way through, in steam rather than over direct heat. In the more conventional pit-barbecue method the outside of the meat is often grilled hard while the inside remains almost raw. (I have since learned that the steam method was once commonly used in England, in Yorkshire.)

There had once been barbecue pans such as our prospective cook described in use in various nearby towns but that was some years ago and presumably they had been destroyed. I thought it worth the effort to try to find them, however, and pressed him for details. One set, he said, had been stored in a barn in East Wallingford. Another had been used for a company picnic at a machine shop in Windsor and might still be around. A third had been used regularly at Tunbridge Fair but he knew these had been burned out.

"If we find the pans," I asked him, "will you cook for us?"

"Well," he said, "I couldn't do it alone." Then he explained that the man who had invented this method of barbecuing lived in South Woodstock, if we wanted to look him up. If Gene would consent, so would he.

So, sloshing through the rain, trying to avoid the drip down the back of my neck from the leaky roof, and stopping every few miles to refill the radiator, we went on to South Woodstock. I inquired at the general store if they knew Gene Rhodes.

"Gene? Sure."

"Where could we find him?"

"Hey, Jimmy, seen Gene today?"

"Yeah, he's at the big house."

So we were directed to the big house.

The big house turned out to be a magnificent old brick structure of the federal period that Mr. Rhodes had bought and was restoring, an activity that was part hobby and part profession, and his more than seventy-five years didn't seem to constitute a handicap. As we drove into the yard we heard the sound of hammers and saws and when we stopped, a tall, thin gentleman with sharp grey eyes and a stoop came from the shed.

We greeted one another and I took my time stating my errand because it was fun talking with this man. I finally asked him if he would cook for us. Again there was the question of pans. Would he cook for us if we found the pans?

"Yes," he said. "I guess I might."

Then he showed me through the house and we talked of restorations, wall stencils, panelling, and other matters far more interesting than barbecues.

In South Woodstock we were not far from my brother's place so by the way of wet, mushy back roads we proceeded there. I think it was the prospect of a moment's relaxation in a warm, dry kitchen that provided the lure. My brother ran an informal kind of inn at the time and greeted us at the kitchen door with flour on his hands and a big grin on his face. He was making doughnuts. He had learned to cook as a boy scout in Switzerland and always enjoyed it. So we relieved him of some of the product of his labor and a cup of tea for me, discussed barbecue pans, invited him and his guests to join us on the appointed day, and went home, still in the rain.

It was raining harder than ever a day or so later when my husband took the old car and searched for the pans that were said to be in East Wallingford. He found the barn where they had been stored all right, but a bunch of Tom Sawyers and Huck Finns had found them first and they were no longer usable.

It was still raining the day after that when we both set out to try to find the pans used for the company picnic at Windsor. No one at the machine shop seemed ever to have heard of the event until an elderly employee recalled that pans such as we described had been turned over to the Elks Club at Newport in New Hampshire. We thanked the man and drove to Newport but inquiries at the Elks Club drew a blank.

We were now fairly discouraged and also very wet and tired. On the way home my husband decided that new pans would have to be made. So we stopped at the local hardware-and-plumbing store and put the matter to them. Here were sympathetic ears. We drew pictures and diagrams, they considered the materials they had on hand or could get. An evaporator from a sugar rig would do for the bottom pan. The top one could be made without much trouble. The great hood would be a little harder to put together but it could be done. In fact, our friends dropped everything and did it, and only charged for the materials.

Meanwhile, of course, we had been working on the rest
of the menu and getting people to take over the various items
on it. There would be boiled potatoes, vegetable salad (my
job), bread and butter, coffee, and ice cream. A line of serving
tables would have to be built in the pasture. To eat, people
would sit on the ground or on logs or rocks, as they found
them—a semi-circle of woods bordering the pasture and
the normal supply of rocky knolls and hillocks were available for this purpose. The customers would bring their own
knives, forks, and spoons.

One Sunday afternoon, under the direction of the co-chairman, who was also carpenter and stone mason, a group of us
built the tables and the arches over which the beef, the
potatoes, and the coffee would be cooked. Someone, I think
it was the treasurer, brought a milk bottle of martinis, which
helped. A parking lot was arranged. The local constable was
invited to keep an eye on law and order, but this proved an
unnecessary precaution and after that first barbecue we never
again thought of asking for an officer of the law to be present.
The young man who worked our farm was a devotee of hill-
billy and cowboy music and he arranged for entertainers in
that genre to perform on the platform of our farm truck.
Somewhere he also managed to get a portable generator,
microphone, and amplifier for the occasion.

Meanwhile, to our distress, it kept right on raining. Not just
a drizzle or a shower, but honest rain. The barbecue was to be
held on a Sunday and preparations would start the day before.
The cooks arrived at the pasture on Saturday at about noon
and rigged a tarp over one of the tables. Someone fetched
the beef in a pickup and the cooks went to work on the
carcass. At their direction I had provided the dressing: fifty

loaves of stale bread, five pounds of salt pork, a sack of onions, boxes of spices and seasoning. I took all this over to the pasture. The cooks dumped the bread, which I had broken up, into two big galvanized wash tubs and added the salt pork cut in small pieces. By this time a number of helpers had gathered and we set about peeling and dicing onions, the effect on the tear ducts being on a massive scale. The onions were added to the tubs. Then the cooks poured in the seasonings, Gene added some herbs from his own garden, the whole of it was mixed with a little water to the right texture, then transferred to the carcass, and the opening secured with skewers. After that we peeled several bushels of potatoes and tossed them into milk cans filled with water to keep them fresh until the following day.

By the time the beef was stuffed and trussed the rain had stopped. The meat was transferred to the roasting pan on a rack that looked like a stretcher slung with wires instead of canvas. Water was added to the lower pan. The hood was lowered into place. The fire in the arch was started, steam began to generate and the beef began to cook, a process that was to continue for some eighteen hours before the head chef pronounced it done. A small sliding door in the front end of the hood allowed him to poke the beef with a fork tied to a long stick to test for doneness.

When a pleasant sunset appeared we began to have hopes for a dry day on the morrow. And hope we needed. We had planned to sell most of our tickets beforehand but not many had been taken and we were in for a total expense of something like $300, including the cost of the pans. Country folk are cautious and in this case they wanted to be sure how things were going—the promised barbecue, which was a new venture, and the weather—before they committed themselves to the price of a ticket. In those days a dollar was still pretty much a dollar.

As the weather cleared in the late afternoon, more people from the neighborhood and also from town gathered in the pasture for a picnic supper, or just for refreshments. Gene produced a bottle of rum and one of Bourbon, someone else had brought a gallon of hard cider, and there were other contributions. Pretty soon the party began to be quite gay. We built a big bonfire and sat around it and talked and sang. The cooks were to spend the night tending the beef, keeping water in the nether pan, and feeding the fire. It was one o'clock in the morning before the last of the would-be assistant cooks departed and the cooks themselves settled down to what remained of the night.

On the following morning, dawn announced one of the loveliest days of the summer. The sun came up and, together with a balmy breeze, dried the wet terrain. At six o'clock my husband relieved the cooks to give them a chance to rest. Soon there was a bustle of people getting the auxiliary parts of the meal ready: boiling potatoes, making salad, arranging bread and butter, preparing to make gallons of coffee, and attending to other last-minute matters.

By 12:30, much to our relief, a good crowd had gathered and the ceremony of depanning the beef took place. Six men removed the great hood from the pans, then carefully lifted the beef, all in one piece on its stretcher, from the top pan and cautiously transferred it to the table at the head of the serving line. This not without a good deal of huffing and puffing, however (it weighed three hundred pounds), and much wondering on my part whether the transfer would be

177

a safe one, so tender did the meat seem. Once the burden was safely placed on the table, the stretcher wires and poles were removed, and four carvers—the two cooks, the hardware man, and my husband—moved into place. I rang the dinner bell and the line of waiting people started through.

An hour later everyone had been served—nearly three hundred customers—and the beef was reduced to a pile of bones. Those of us who stood behind the line of serving tables to fill the plates as they were presented to us soon discovered that it was an advantageous position because the carvers favored us and some of the choicest tenderloin found its way in our direction. We also discovered the difference, when it came to potatoes, between a city person and a farmer: the first will draw his plate away after one serving but a farmer keeps his plate steady until two or even three helpings have been transferred to it.

The only major mistake that first year was to provide paper plates which tended to wilt under the load of food we piled on them. Only one man, my friend the blacksmith-philosopher, had had the wit to bring his own plate. In the following years we asked the customers to bring their own, and we came to recognize the barbecue old hand from the novice by the kind of plate he brought. The really sophisticated offered big pie plates or, the best of all, divided plastic trays; the novice brought a small plate or one of paper. Abandoning the use of paper plates also eased the task of picking up the pasture at the end of the day, although that never was much of a problem because most people burned their trash in one of the arches before leaving the grounds.

In subsequent years we also improved on the menu. Our friend Mr. Bostwick who provided the beef insisted that instead of boiled potatoes we should have mashed potatoes with a big pat of butter in the middle of each serving, and he gave us ten pounds of his own butter to make sure of it. The mashing was done by a crew of boys armed with sap buckets, mashers, and cans of evaporated milk. We also substituted coleslaw for vegetable or lettuce salad because it was easier to make after we discovered we could use the institution-sized slicer in the Aggie school's kitchen. At the last barbecue, held in that summer of 1952, so adept had we become that we even made thickened gravy to serve with the potatoes and dressing. But in all the seven years we put the barbecue on, we never changed the price of the meal; to the end it remained one dollar, and half-price for children.

As for the financial returns of the enterprise, on the first occasion, when we had the help of eighteen dollars from a passed hat, we broke even. After that we accumulated a little reserve against a rainy day—which never came—and when profits began to show up we turned them over to one of the children's aid societies in the state.

After the meal when everyone had eaten as much as he could—even seconds if he had the capacity—there was entertainment, and only that first year was it professional. Sometimes there was community singing, generally there were games and contests, and amateur music. At the last few barbecues there was folk dancing and singing by a group of young people who called themselves Old Joe Clark's Gang by reason of the fact that they all lived cooperatively in an old house on Beacon Hill in Boston that had once belonged to one Joseph Clark, whose nameplate remained on the door. The Gang came on from Boston each August to visit a former member of the group who was now a local farmer, and they soon became a regular part of the barbecue. In addition to providing entertainment on the day itself they also helped with preparations on Saturday and enlivened the gathering that evening around the big bonfire with music and songs and stories until midnight or after. Then most of them crawled into sleeping bags in the surrounding woods and the rest of us drove home for a night more comfortable, perhaps, but less starry.

Part of the fun of the barbecue was the fact that it was largely a local and family affair. Although a good many summer people always attended because, for economic reasons, we advertised in surrounding towns, it was the local farmers, and the townspeople and their families who were most prominently represented. It was for this reason also that the affair always wound up in time for the men folk to get home for evening chores. Usually by five o'clock the guests were gone, the fires were nearly out, and the few of us who remained went over the pasture collecting what debris there was and burning it. Our farm truck, loaded with pots and pans and other equipment, was always the last to leave the grounds.

The day after the first barbecue, which had been so lovely, the rain set in again and stayed with us for more than a week. The Lord had been good to us, this in contrast to His behavior on the occasion of a certain church supper and fair we once attended. Part of that had to be held out of doors and the rains came at just the wrong moment. It did seem a pity, said a little old gentleman to me, that they could not have had better weather, especially considering the nature of the affair. Our barbecue's only claim to Heavenly favor was its friendly and neighborly character. Whether for this or some other reason, at every barbecue the weather was fine. Once it was fearfully hot and humid, and on the last one the rain threatened to drown us the day before, but perhaps because we pitched a couple of big army tents that afternoon, the skies cleared before evening and the next day was fair.

For seven consecutive years the barbecue was put on under the direction of two people, whoever was willing to do the job or could be persuaded to do it. I did it two or three times, my sister Sid did it once or twice, and two other women and two or three men took turns as chairman or co-chairman. But it was hard work and those who had helped during the early years were not always available for later ones. In the end, although support for the venture continued and even increased among the customers, it was hard to get enough people with enough time to give to the project and in 1952 it was held for the last time. However, the pans are still stored in our barn and perhaps some day the Christian Hill Barbecue will be revived.

*   *   *

During this period in our lives the family exchequer was in pretty fair shape so regardless of continuing college expenses for the older children we planned to stay on the farm and were able to prepare for the coming winter with a pleasant feeling of permanence. By this time too our activities in the community had become important to us. Normally we are non-joiners but in our home community we happily became members of all kinds of groups. My husband belongs to Rotary and the Men's Brotherhood and is a deacon of the United Church. I belong to the local chapter of the AAUW, the Women's Club, and the women's auxiliary of the United Church.

It was during this fall that I had my first—and probably

my last—experience as chairman of a committee to put on a church supper. I had never done such a thing before, having always limited my activities in the church kitchen to washing dishes. But it seemed as though I should take my turn and the ladies thought so, too. I warned them that I was no great hand at such matters but perhaps my connection with the barbecue gave them an unwarranted optimism. In any case, I finally agreed and they agreed to help.

The main dish was to be baked ham and four hams were ordered from a local merchant and delivered to the church kitchen. Lovely Vermont hams, they were, cured with maple sugar instead of molasses. I prepared them with a coating of brown sugar and mustard, decorated them with cloves, and when the time came, put them in the two big ovens.

Pretty soon my assistants (bosses) arrived to prepare vegetables and other fixings. I checked my ovens from time to time but just at the wrong moment I forgot about them and when next I opened them, clouds of blue smoke came forth. It was the sugar coating on the hams that had burned. The ladies were very nice about the whole thing and the carvers did the best they could with what was presented to them on the big cutting boards. But I was chagrined and I think my failure confirmed the ladies in their opinion that I was just a big-city girl after all.

The day had been a mild one in November, by evening it was raining, and at midnight when we drove home a heavy wet snow was falling. There was nearly eight inches of snow on the ground the next morning and snow was still coming down. I would gladly have stayed home to enjoy it but had arranged to return to the church kitchen to help clean up. I started out after breakfast. Although the jeep wagon was only a two-wheel-drive affair, the going wasn't too bad until I reached a stretch of road that winds through woods where the heavy snow clinging to small trees and saplings made them bend over to form a thick white tunnel. Some of the laden boughs were so low I couldn't see the road beyond them and had to buck the car through them, then stop and clean the windshield before going on to the next obstacle. Fortunately it wasn't very cold and the spectacle of the heavy clinging snow on every branch was a marvelous display, combining secrecy and remoteness with beauty in a manner that kept me from thinking too much about the possibility of getting really stuck and no immediate chance of rescue.

The snow fell all day, while I worked in the church kitchen. I've always wanted to be snowed in on the farm. As a child on my father's farm in Connecticut I had had that experience more than once and it was always a lovely one. There is something warm and snug and safe-feeling about sitting beside an open fire with the snow falling outside and gradually forming a lovely deep white barrier between you and the rest of the world. Always provided, of course, that the larder and the woodshed are well stocked, as ours were. In the days before the home freezer there were cured hams and bacon, eggs in water glass, a constant supply of milk from the barn, and pantry shelves loaded with home-canned fruits and vegetables, jars of jam and jelly and pickles and relishes, and frames of honey.

But today the likelihood of being snowbound has all but disappeared. For one thing, there doesn't seem to be as much snow. For another, the roads are better and they are better plowed after a storm. And even if there is a delay in that operation, there is the jeep.

So, although we've never been snowed in on the farm, the day I helped clean up the church kitchen I did have the experience of being snowed out. On the way home that day I wasn't surprised to find that the jeep wagon couldn't make the first long hill off the blacktop; halfway up it lost traction. So I backed down to the blacktop again (the wagon didn't have that fatal passion for ditches that distinguished the Olds), and made a long detour to the village, only a mile from us, where the children were in school. The man who worked our place at the time had a Universal Jeep, three of the children were his, and there was Davis. I expected the jeep would be down to fetch them and I would get a lift home.

So leaving the car in a friendly yard I sat on a bench at the back of the schoolroom for an hour or more and watched the teacher as she moved from one grade to another among the twenty or so pupils who occupied the one room and ranged in ages from six to fourteen. Somewhat nostalgically, I recalled my own early years in a similar school. There was a big iron stove in one corner of the room around which caps and mittens and socks and boots were set to dry, giving off the unmistakable smell of a one-room schoolhouse in winter. It was warm and comfortable in there, while outside the snow continued falling.

When school let out, the children and I waited for a while but no jeep appeared so we set out to walk home. Although the distance was only a mile, it was all uphill with part of it around a sharp steep grade called the Oxbow. I took the lead of the column, followed by the oldest boy, and the littlest girl brought up the rear in order to have a well-broken path.

Fortunately it was still mild, and in the growing dusk, with the snow falling in the fading light, it was more beautiful

184

than ever. In addition, there was the silence, made deeper by the nearly imperceptible sound that snow, if it is a little wet, makes as it falls—the sum of millions of light contacts between snowflake and twig or branch, and between snowflake and snowflake as they meet on the snow-covered ground. The memory of that walk stays with me. Perhaps it is one of the reasons that Davis too, loves the snow so well.

CHAPTER 12

Turkey and The Thames

WE HAD BEEN UNINTERRUPTEDLY ON THE FARM FOR ABOUT a year, going happily about our business, when my husband received a second invitation to teach the spring semester at the University of Puerto Rico. Although winter in Vermont is our favorite season there, this one had started with a good deal of vigor and it wasn't hard to accept the invitation. So, having spent most of one cold January morning getting the jeep wagon out of a snow drift on the Oxbow, two days later we were lying in the sun beside a beautiful pool in San Juan.

It was during this visit to the Island that my husband was asked by the United Nations to go to Turkey as chief of a mission to set up an institute of public administration at the University of Ankara and at the same time to head the UN technical assistance program in Turkey. On top of this came yet another invitation, this one to spend three months in England at the Administrative Staff College at Henley-on-Thames. We were familiar with England but knew nothing at all about Turkey and the more we read the more interesting it sounded and so did the work for the UN. It seemed possible to fit the Turkish and English assignments together and this we did, though it meant a total stay abroad of something like fifteen months.

Late in May we wound up the semester in Puerto Rico and returned to the farm where we spent a rather hectic summer preparing for a departure which, on this occasion, was complicated by the need for security clearance, for a draft of lectures to be delivered at the University of Ankara, and for an inordinate amount of luggage.

When all was ready we boarded a big Pan Am plane that took off from New York early one evening and set us down in London in time for lunch the following day. We spent the afternoon shopping and exploring and next morning resumed our journey to the east. We skirted the Alps on the north just as the sun went down behind the snowcaps of Switzerland and turned that country into a landscape of pink and gold. We arrived at Istanbul in time for a late dinner. The city seemed big and confusing and we were glad to leave it the next day, although the battered little Dakota plane that took us to Ankara was so old there were holes in the floor through which we could see the landscape of Anatolia below.

In Ankara our hotel was close to the old part of the city, which dates back nearly 5000 years to the time of the Hittites. The new part, as we were to discover, looks a good deal like Washington, D.C., with much the same kind of construction boom in government buildings and apartment houses that characterized Washington after World War II. We also found that most Americans in Ankara—there were something like 2000 of them at the time, mostly service people—lived in the newest residential area along with members of the diplomatic corps. Although we were Americans, we were in Turkey on a United Nations mission to the Turkish people and did not feel like clanning up with other Americans in what has come to be called in many foreign cities, the Golden Ghetto. So we looked for living quarters elsewhere and soon found a big moderately priced apartment in a convenient location.

The apartment was furnished but that meant, quite literally, only furniture. No equipment. So in addition to what we had brought we also needed such essentials as china, glass, and kitchen ware. Knowing this, the wife of the Dean of the Political Science Faculty at the University offered to help me in my shopping, pointing out that in a nation where all purchases are made on the basis of a bargain, she had better do the bargaining. No expert at this myself, I gratefully agreed.

She is a most remarkable lady. In addition to having studied in four or five European countries including Sweden and learning the language in each, she had spent a year at the University of Minnesota doing postgraduate work, and she also had a law degree and a practice in Ankara. She was to be my husband's interpreter in his lectures at the Institute, and on the side, if that is what it could be called, she was studying for a Ph.D. from the University of Ankara. Finally, of course, she ran her household and entertained for her husband who is one of the most distinguished men in Turkey.

The morning of the day we were to move to the apartment, Nermin met me at the hotel and we set out, armed with a long list and plenty of money. Our first stop was a small shop where the only dishes made in Turkey are sold. More pottery than china, they are lovely and colorful to look at, brittle to use, and inexpensive to replace. The proprietor offered us the tiny cups of coffee without which no serious business is approached in Turkey. "A cup of coffee is worth forty years of friendship," is the saying, and we sipped as I made my selections and my friend made my purchases.

After an hour or so of this kind of shopping up and down the streets of the old town we were both loaded with bundles and packages and had hired a small boy with a big basket on his back to take more. We returned to the hotel at noon, discharged our loot, had lunch with my husband and Davis, and set out again. This time we concentrated on food, most of which was purchased from small specialized shops surrounding an open area and constituting a permanent, semi-arcaded market. Meat in one shop, poultry in another, groceries in a third, tea and coffee in a fourth, cheese, butter, olives, and olive oil in a fifth, fruit and vegetables in a sixth, and spices in a shop that smelled like nothing I had ever imagined before.

In the open area in the center of the market were temporary stalls for the vendors of flowers, plants, baskets, and other miscellany. I have a weakness for baskets and with bundles piling up in my arms, I naturally had an immediate need for at least one. It was a good excuse and I took advantage of it. We hired another pack boy and filled his basket, too. Then just as we were about to leave, my guide spotted an ironing board in one of the stalls at a price that seemed like a bargain. She couldn't resist it, though by that time I, for my part, would gladly have passed it up. But she bought it, tucked it under her arm along with a bundle of coat hangers and a bag of oranges, and we marched back down the hill to the hotel.

Perhaps I don't need to say that all of this shopping was accomplished on foot. I am tall and a fast walker, but my friend was faster and more energetic than I. I had the feeling that we had been caught up in a whirlwind, and to judge by the quantity and mixed character of our plunder, so we had. At the hotel we filled two taxis with family, luggage, loot, and guide, proceeded to the apartment where our guide took a quick look around to see that nothing was lacking, and then listed her phone number in our book.

"I think," she said as she prepared to leave, "that you should have a chance to eat turkey in Turkey. Will you have Thanksgiving dinner with us next week?"

We accepted with enthusiasm. She then wished us well and disappeared about her own business, of which she must have had at least a day's-worth ahead of her and it was now mid-afternoon.

As for me, I am used to unpacking quickly. By evening we were comfortably settled and had dinner in our own dining room. A marvelous room it was, too, connected by an archway with the living room and dominated by two enormous elaborate mahogany sideboards, bepillared, bemarbled, bemirrored, bebrasshandled, and bedoilied. I dispensed only with the doilies, all betasseled as they were.

The next thing was to enter Davis in a school maintained by the American Army for the benefit of the nearly nine hundred children of American service personnel who were then living in Ankara. Davis was in third grade but it was his fifth school and it was here that he got over the hump in adjusting to new schools. His first day in class in Ankara was dreadfully unhappy; even his teacher felt for him in his misery and told me so. I tried to comfort him and he never asked to stay home. At the end of the first week I saw that things were going better and asked him about it.

"You know, Mom," he said, "the first day in a new school

is terrible. The second day is a little better. The third day isn't
so bad."

It was a good school and he did well.

*   *   *

It is odd how quickly one feels at home in Turkey. Or
maybe it isn't. Maybe the sophisticated simplicity of the
people and their ways has a universal appeal. In any case, here
is a strange land about which most Westerners know little.
Though familiar to us from ancient-history courses as Asia
Minor, I doubt if many Americans make the connection between that land and modern Turkey. We've heard of the
legendary Terrible Turk, of Atatürk and his reforms, and
that Turkey is a member of NATO. But what else?

The Turkish language is related to no European language
with the exception of Hungarian and Finnish; it is highly
agglutinated and difficult for a Westerner to learn. The re-
ligion is Muslim and to some extent governs food and drink
customs, clothing for women, and shoes for both sexes. It
also influences sounds; five times each day the muezzin is
proclaimed in song from the balcony of the minaret that is a
part of every mosque, and in a city there are many mosques.
This call to prayer is traditionally sung by an imam standing
on the high balcony, but increasingly now, so we were told,
it is broadcast by the imam from the base of the minaret and
spread to his flock by a loudspeaker on the balcony. We soon
got used to hearing the haunting tones of the muezzin at very
early hours of the morning.

The sights on the streets of a Turkish city are new to people
like Americans. Peasants in their native dress are strikingly
colorful, especially in the case of women who have discarded

the black mantle that covers everything but the eyes; most townspeople, however, wear Western clothing or, in the case of some of the men, a modification thereof in which the pants have a kind of bloomer-seat. In the old part of Ankara, called Ulus, there are many more horses, donkeys, and shaggy little burrows than there are automobiles and trucks. When even these animals are lacking as means of transport, there is always a man's back and amazingly bulky loads are sometimes carried that way. Then there are the smells encountered in the street—the aroma of freshly ground coffee, of tea, nuts, spices, fresh bread, and pastry as one passes the shops that sell these wares.

Much Turkish cooking is oriental in origin and all of it is wonderful. Lamb is the great staple meat but there is also beef, poultry, and fish. Then there are yogurt, cheeses made of cow's, goat's, or sheep's milk, olives and olive oil, nuts, honey, rice in great quantities and cooked in two or three dozen ways, eggplant in an equal variety of recipes, leeks as thick as a man's wrist, and all of them delectable. A liquor called raki which tastes like anise and, when mixed with water, looks like thin milk, is the main Turkish drink, but there is also vodka, gin, liqueurs, and wine, all plentiful and reasonably priced. Crusty bread made after the French fashion can be bought at the bakery right from the oven. In season, fruits surpass in variety and flavor anything I have ever seen—strawberries, melons of all kinds, peaches, apricots, plums, six or seven varieties of cherries and grapes—finally, the ripe figs, so tender one can eat them skin and all, picked near Izmir before sunup with the dew still on them and flown to Ankara to be eaten the same day.

Yet with all this, for us the outstanding feature of Turkey was the people: intelligent, intellectually curious, active, inventive, quick-moving, friendly, and helpful. And courteous and considerate and courtly—the list could go on and on. Perhaps the thing that brings them closest to Americans is that the modern Turk is a pioneer. Turkey is an ancient land, it doesn't need, as America did, to be discovered and settled. The pioneering now going on there is in the realm of economic and political development, and the same spirit serves to this end that served to implement Manifest Destiny on the prairies and plains of America. For all these reasons, and despite the language barrier, in just a few days we began to feel perfectly at home wherever we went.

As United Nations personnel, we were denied access to the United States post exchange used by service personnel, and hence did all our shopping in the local stores. This introduced us to all kinds of local wares that shoppers at the PX missed, and for my part the only item I missed was facial tissues and I made do with toilet paper instead. The only local item that I never could bring myself to buy was a sheep's head, though my butcher tried hard to overcome my distaste for it by practically giving it to me. Cheese made from sheep's milk and stuffed into the skin of a lamb, however, didn't bother me at all.

In the food markets and the shops and among the peddlers who sold fruit from door to door, every merchant carried a pencil behind his ear and had a piece of paper handy. So, after a while, did I. I would ask the price of what was offered, the merchant would write it down, I would refuse with the correct disdainful lift of the head (the negative gesture) and write a counter-offer, and after several such exchanges an agreement would be happily reached. I found that if I really wanted something, the merchant generally got the better of me, but if I didn't especially want it, I would get the better of him, though I was always a little surprised when this happened; rather pleased, too.

When the strawberry season came on in June, however, I forgot all about bargaining and paid any price that was asked because strawberries are another weakness of mine and these, shipped from Istanbul in two-pound boxes, were absolutely the most delicious I've ever tasted. Day after day for two or three weeks I bought them and ate them plain or with yogurt and a little honey dribbled over them. The rest of the family could take them or leave them, but I never had enough. They nearly did me in more than once because I don't believe in washing all the flavor out of berries with great floods of water before eating them—a little water will do, I always hope. But a bottle of pills that I kept on the dining table, primarily for Davis but also on occasion for other members of the family, generally had me ready for the next batch of berries.

Only once did I lose a bargain and really regret it, though more for the humiliation it caused me than for the price I paid. My husband had seen a coffee roaster, a simple little gadget that could be bought, he learned, in the old part of town for something less than a lira, at that time worth about thirty-five cents. So one day when I was shopping in Ulus I searched for a coffee roaster, managed to make my requirement known, and was escorted by a volunteer guide down a narrow side street to what looked like a blacksmith shop without the horses. The nature of my errand was conveyed to the smith who reached up into the low rafters and took down the very item I wanted.

I asked the price and was told four liras, which was about five times the right price. But four liras was still not a great

sum and I didn't feel like bargaining. My mistake. I knew
I should have and my guide and the smith were obviously
waiting for the customary incredulous lift of the head. But
instead I paid the four liras and their surprise was immediately
apparent. I put the gadget in my tote bag whence, being long
and a bit awkward, it protruded at some length. My guide
followed me back to the main street laughing behind my back
in a most uproarious and to me, unseemly fashion, apparently
telling his friends what this crazy American woman had done
and slapping his thighs in merriment while I walked off down
the street trying to look as though I didn't understand what
was going on and certainly failing. I still have the coffee
roaster, though, and even use it now and then.

*   *   *

One of the aspects of life in Turkey that we enjoyed most
was the social intercourse with Turks whom we came to
know as the result of my husband's work. For the most part
these were government officials and professors and their
families. To dine in the home of a Turk and to carry on a
dinner conversation with him and his guests is to eat super-
lative food and to participate in discussion ranging over an
infinitely varied area of intellectual subject matter. Many of
our dinner companions spoke excellent English or French or
German or all three in addition to Turkish and communication
was never a problem. The houses and apartments were sometimes small, especially if they were new, but all had a double
drawing room (in the old days the ladies sat apart from the
gentlemen, and though the custom has largely disappeared
the facilities remain) and were luxuriously furnished with
fine oriental rugs, silk draperies, mahogany furniture, and

French porcelain. The men were well tailored, the women dressed in the best that Vienna and Paris and Rome can offer, the food and drink exotic and wonderful, the talk intellectually stimulating and spiced with wit and charm and understanding.

On one occasion we were invited to dine at the home of a prominent member of the political opposition. We arrived at what appeared to be a small house, one of a row of attached houses with a path leading through a small yard to the front door that had nothing to distinguish it from its neighbors. Our host greeted us in a bare narrow hall and we left our wraps in a small anteroom. Then we were escorted through a door at the back of the hall to enter a large L-shaped room, beautiful in its proportions and furnished in the oriental fashion with rich hangings, luxurious Turkish rugs, bright silken cushions, marvelous hand-woven and embroidered materials, inlaid furniture, copper, brass, objets d'art, ceramics, delicate porcelain, paintings, and a library of books in many languages.

Dinner was a buffet arrangement and the main decoration on the long shining table was a big copper tray piled high with Seckel pears—about a bushel of them. The meal began with bouillon served in exquisite Limoges cups. Among the courses that followed we were introduced to bulgur, which is kernels of wheat, cracked, pre-cooked, dried, and then cooked again like rice. The meal concluded with rich honey-and-almond pastries, fruits, and Turkish coffee. We ate leisurely in congenial groups to the accompaniment of wine and good conversation.

Afterwards our host explained to me that as a politician he had to see all kinds of people and generally received them in the anteroom off the hall. He spoke not as a snob but as one who cherished his privacy. Only his personal friends knew of this room. There was also a garden beyond, but it was night and we couldn't see it.

Here then was the private world of a cultivated, wealthy, and realistic man taking an active part in the affairs of a nation currently concerned with very realistic matters indeed— and occasionally because of his opposition views, going to prison for his pains. Perhaps it is the virtue of a Turk to be realistic and at the same time to be able to enjoy other aspects of life that are compounded of large amounts of imagination as well—the parts of his life that are intellectual, sentimental, hedonistic, artistic, even unreal when judged by the standards of the public part of his life.

Having two jobs in Turkey, my husband's time was pretty well taken up so we didn't see as much of the country as we'd have liked. The trips we did make, usually under the auspices of the Turkish Department of Agriculture, were exciting and instructive. Provided with an official car, a driver, and an interpreter, we explored part of the southern coast where cotton is the main crop, and part of the northern coast along the Black Sea (such swimming!) where forestry is prominent, along with corn, tobacco, and tea.

Most interesting of all was a weekend visit to the native village of our friend the Dean of the Political Science Faculty at the University; many close members of his family still lived there. Situated on a small plateau far off the main highway and surrounded by broad pastures and fields of grain, this village is the home of some fifty families. Like many other aspects of the Turkish economy and culture, it was in the process of passing quickly from a primitive type of life to a more complex one, skipping some of the intermediate steps altogether. Thus, with fifty families, there was no telephone, no telegraph, only one radio, and no automobiles—but there were twenty-five tractors.

The villagers received us with all the rites of welcome and hospitality due the friends of a distinguished native son. We were made to feel *en famille*. The next day we were taken to visit several other homes in the village, shown the farming arrangements, a government stud barn, and a community plantation of young trees, while Davis stayed behind and played marbles with a group of boys of his own age in the courtyard of the homestead we were visiting. On bidding us goodbye men and women alike embraced us; it is the traditional farewell gesture. My husband and I have often thought that to retire to such a village and write would be a rewarding experience; the life would be easy and friendly and free and totally without interruption. A vacant homestead, partly in ruins, caught our eye—and our imagination.

Scattered episodes that I remember from our travels in Turkey include receiving a bunch of violets from the principal of an agricultural school; being one of only two women among ten men at a nightclub dinner (Turkish women do not ordinarily attend such affairs) that started at eight and didn't end until after midnight; watching Davis take out after a cat on the site of the chapel of Saint Paul in Ephesus and tripping and skinning his chin; out in a small boat on the Black Sea buying fish and melons from other boats and then eating them that night at a guest house maintained by a big lumber company on the edge of a forest; being scared speechless on a wild ride by jeep over mountainous logging trails in that same forest; being terrified by the habit of some Turkish drivers of following hard on the wheels of the car ahead at 120 kilometers an hour, and their wretched custom of dousing their headlights at night when approaching another car, the other driver doing the same until they are "safely" past one another; and finally, the indescribable expression on the face of a little high-stepping Arabian mare as, without turning her head, she watched her trainer and caught his signals and the words, "my daughter," with which he persuaded her to obedience.

I had a good deal of leisure in Ankara and made the most of it by writing a little and reading quite a lot just for fun. A maid came every day to do dishes, cleaning, laundry, ironing, and some of the cooking. I also did some sewing as ready-made clothing, especially for a tall gal, was scarce. Once I had a pair of shoes made to order but they were a failure. I chose the model and the leather but when the cobbler took the measurements of my foot he couldn't believe the evidence of his tape.

"Surely not!" he exclaimed. "This is impossible!"

So he took a centimeter off the length of the shoes and I never could wear them with comfort. Fortunately they were not expensive.

Davis continued happily at the American school but his preferred playmates were Turkish. A vacant and not very clean lot on our street was headquarters for something like thirty boys in our immediate vicinity, ranging in age from six to sixteen. Here they ran the gamut of what boyhood activity could be carried on without the use of running water. Games followed each other in due season, and often the same season as in Western countries: marbles, kites, yoyos, archery, darts, all in the proper sequence. There were groups and group captains and lieutenants, contests, battles, and a circus. In addition, all the young Turks knew about cowboys and stalked and bang-banged away at each other in a manner no different from boys in an American suburb. Equipment, however, was scarce and a toy gun a luxury. A few boys even wore jeans or a cowboy hat, left them, presumably, by some departing American family; the possessors of such items were the envy of all the rest.

Into this situation Davis introduced boxing and baseball, having taken along his gloves and bat. He acted as coach and referee, a good deal of prestige for a third-grader. He also taught his companions some English, though of a kind that their parents probably didn't approve any more than I could approve some of the Turkish words learned by Davis. Coming home one day as a group of boys was playing on the street in front of our house, for example, I heard one of them shout,

"Shueueuet uuuuup!" And then,

"You'rrrre craaaaaaazy!" This combination of familiar words and Turkish intonation was devastating.

For his part, Davis kept his unacceptable Turkish vocabulary mostly to himself, except once when he said something to the maid that caused her to come storming out to the terrace where I was writing, overflowing with explanations I couldn't understand, her feathers all ruffled. Davis was clearly implicated. At first he denied it but finally admitted he had called her a donkey, which to a Turk is like calling a Frenchman a cow. A scolding was administered, an apology offered and accepted, Houriye went back to her work with her feathers smoothed down, Davis returned to his friends, and I to my manuscript.

*   *   *

Not all the travelling we did that year was in Turkey. My mother was spending the winter as usual in Switzerland and I made two trips to be with her at strategic moments. One was her seventieth birthday, the last day in the year and a cold wet one in that part of the world. But we did have a good time and I was sorry to leave her. The second was the following June to get her packed and put safely aboard a ship at Genoa. She had had a slight stroke in the spring and I was not optimistic about the future, nor, I think, was she. She wanted to get home and although she had rented an apartment in Vevey to return to at the end of the summer, I don't think she really expected to occupy it. I said goodbye to her—for the last time, it was to turn out—on the S. S. *Independence*, a ship suitably named for the transportation of a lady such as she.

Later that summer my husband was called to Switzerland on official business and he took Davis and me along. We had two lovely weeks in Geneva, Davis learning to ride a bicycle, and I revisiting with my family some of the places there that I had once known and loved. Hardly anything was changed except me. We also had a few days in Rome where Davis learned to operate an elevator at the hotel and to drive a cab horse. The thing he remembers best, however, is losing some Italian coins down a drain grating in the huge plaza in front of St. Peter's.

Back in Turkey, September was approaching and so, too, the end of my husband's mission. But in my memory that period is dominated by the news of my mother's illness and then her death. In a daze of shock, I packed—a job further complicated by the possessions we had acquired in Turkey and naturally wanted to take home: pottery, dishes, baskets, copper, brass, two rugs, several goats'-hair blankets, books, the coffee roaster that had cost me so much humiliation, a pony harness, and more.

Finally everything was ready. The little Dakota took us to Istanbul where we spent a day and a night with Turkish friends on one of the Princes' Islands in the Marmora Sea. The next morning we left the island early, had breakfast on the ferry, enplaned at the airport, had lunch aloft somewhere over Yugoslavia, had dinner aloft after leaving Copenhagen, and were met by a friend at Stockholm airport at ten o'clock in time to settle down for a good night's sleep at a comfortable hotel.

The reason for going to Sweden was to allow my husband to participate in the final examination—an extraordinarily formal occasion—of a candidate for a Ph.D. degree, a man who once had been a student of his at Evanston. We took advantage of the chance to have a short vacation, spending most of it alone on the farm of some friends about forty miles from Stockholm. A cottage beside a lake was surrounded by pastures and forests. After the long hot dry summer in Turkey, the cool moist climate of Sweden was like water to a wilting plant. My men folk fished with gratifying success while I roamed the woods and picked blueberries. We ate on a terrace, and in the cool of the evening sat by a wood fire in the living room; then before going to bed made a trip to the two-holer that differed not at all from the variety with which we were familiar in Vermont.

It was on our return to Stockholm that I inadvertently hurt and shocked my husband by refusing the offer of a fur coat. It was two days before we were to leave for England. He had been generously recompensed for his part in the Ph.D. examination and his expenses also were reimbursed. But the expenses had already been met by us and it was not permitted to take Swedish money out of the country. My husband had been talking for years, off and on, about getting me a fur coat and this seemed to him just the chance.

But I don't like fur coats—great heavy things, expensive to buy and expensive to maintain. So long as the family budget didn't provide for such a luxury the matter had remained an academic one and I had not argued about it but now the problem was suddenly no longer academic, it was real and present.

I tried as tactfully as possible to make my views acceptable but it was useless. My husband is a determined man when aroused, and he was aroused. So after lunch I went with him to the local department store which offered an impressive line of merchandise including fur coats. Then I discovered it was Persian lamb, no less, that he had set his heart on. We had seen the lambs on the hoof in Turkey, and even at the farm in the middle of the plains of Anatolia the skins brought twenty dollars apiece, and they were small skins.

I tried on several Persian lamb coats and several other kinds as well, and fortunately for my side of the deal, all were too short. In the face of mounting frustration my husband made a quick and angry adjustment. He strode out of the store so fast I had to trot to keep up with him. He already knew where the biggest, fanciest, most expensive modern pewter shop in Stockholm was and made a beeline for it. He spent the rest of the afternoon there and came away with a large collection of pewter, his favorite decorative metal. I think he was pleased with the substitution but he swore he'd never again offer me a fur coat and I think he means it.

From Stockholm we flew to England for the three months that my husband was to be associated with the Administrative Staff College at Henley-on-Thames. About half way between London and Oxford, the college occupies an old mansion set amid smooth green lawns and ancient trees on the bank of the Thames. Its function is to train able young executives to be even more able and ready to step into positions of higher responsibility.

As part of my husband's compensation the college provided us with an apartment and a car. Our landlord owned an antiques business and the apartment was furnished accordingly. The college not only added a refrigerator but also stocked it so that when we arrived there was enough food to last a week or more: cooked ham, chicken, and duck; milk from the college's Jersey herd with four inches of cream on top of the bottles; fruits, vegetables, salad greens, cheeses, eggs, butter, jam, marmalade, bread, rolls, coffee, tea, condiments, and a line of canned foods and staples. In the living room and bedroom, the principal's wife had arranged masses of flowers from the college's greenhouses and cutting gardens and she was there when we arrived to greet us. It was a fine welcome.

Davis was enrolled at once in a local private school that he enjoyed from the very first day. I asked him how come.

"In an English school," he explained, "they ask you your name and then they say, 'Come and play.'"

It was as simple as that. I bought him his uniform of grey flannel shorts, grey knee socks, tan blazer, and matching cap and tie. As long as he wore the uniform his manners were English and admirable but as soon as he got home and changed back to jeans, he was a cowboy again. Our landlord's two small children provided companionship and a lovely high-brick-walled garden at the back of the house was a natural playground.

My husband went to work at the college in what were congenial surroundings, human and otherwise. He learned to drive the car on the left side of the road (not hard for him since he is left-handed anyway) and taught me. He spent much of his time at the college and I went back to manuscript.

It was a lovely fall. We took walks in the beech woods, kicking the dry leaves underfoot, and thought of Vermont but were not homesick. We joined the college staff for afternoon tea in the faculty lounge and toasted our feet in front of the open fire. We drove the little car to different parts of England on semi-professional errands and thus visited Oxford, Cambridge, Yorkshire, and the Midlands. Being allergic to big cities, we avoided London as much as possible. (It was not until four years later that I was to fall in love with London in the course of a winter and a spring spent there while my husband was writing a book he contended could be written only in London.)

In England in that fall of 1954 most of the post-war austerity had finally been removed and the shops were loaded with food, native, empire, and imported. We ate the most wonderful beef and mutton in the world, and the best Danish butter. In addition, we encountered a standard of service based on service as a profession that also is the best in the world. And we became acquainted with a form of tolerance based on a dispassionate appraisal of one's adversaries which, at a time of flourishing McCarthyism in the United States, was refreshing indeed.

By mid-December our assignment in England was at an end. We packed—again copiously, since who can resist British woolens?—and took off from London airport on a wet night during a brief break in the fog. Shannon airport for dinner and Irish coffee. Early next morning, New York. At Idlewild our mountain of luggage was such that no inspector would take us on until we insisted, and we didn't blame them. We arrived in Vermont in time to make ready for Christmas with the family.

Mark came on from Washington, Nan from California, my brother and his family from their farm near us, and my sister Sid from Hanover. We sat down to a big dinner in the familiar farm kitchen and soon began to wonder whether we'd ever been away from it at all. Nothing makes one feel at home more quickly than familiar smells, and those created in our kitchen that day were more than adequate.

CHAPTER 13

Of Harness:
Pony and Professional

BEFORE WE LEFT ENGLAND MY HUSBAND HAD BEEN ASKED BY
a foundation in Minneapolis to give a series of courses and
lectures for a group of five or six colleges in that area. The
primary appointment would be to Carleton College which,
with St. Olaf's, is at Northfield just south of the Twin Cities.
It was an attractive offer and my husband accepted.

So, shortly after our brief Christmas holiday at the farm,
we turned in our old jeep wagon on a new one that had four-
wheel drive and two transmissions, loaded it to the roof with
the usual typewriters, books, files, papers, and a few suitcases,
closed the house, and drove out to the lovely little town of
Northfield, arriving there at the end of January in time for
the second semester.

Northfield looks for all the world like a New England town
but proclaims itself, with midwestern assurance, as known for
its "Cows, Colleges, and Contentment." We moved into a big
house that turned out to be quite a house in other respects

than just size. One could live in it for a long time, for example, without exhausting the resources of its library, which seemed to cover nearly every subject in which a lay person could conceivably have an interest, and in several languages at that. On the material side, the furnace was of the automatic natural gas variety, so despite the cold winter winds and snows that howled outside (and this being Minnesota, they did howl), we were always warm indoors. There was a fireplace in the living room and a study for me in what had once been a morning room. A sun porch and a sleeping porch gave promise of additional pleasure, come spring. So did a garden.

We enrolled Davis in fourth grade at the local public school and discovered how sophisticated he had become in the matter of new schools. He had had enough practice, of course, since this was his seventh and he had attended three of them twice. We called on the principal, were assigned to a classroom, and introduced to the teacher. Davis took a quick look at the classroom from the hall as we passed the door.

"Humph," he remarked. "Wrong desks."

The teacher showed him where to hang his coat in the hall. He divested himself, and then—

"So long, Mom," he said, and followed the teacher into the classroom. That was that.

Two days later Davis announced that he had set up a birthday party for himself (he was to be nine), gave me the guest list and the home phone numbers and asked me to call the mothers, which I did. It was a good party and initiated a series of pleasant boyhood friendships.

My husband's lectures and teaching also proved to be interesting and it was fun visiting the other colleges on the circuit for occasional lectures. My own time was mostly spent in catching up on recent history. In Turkey we had had hardly any outside news and in England hardly any that touched us very closely. But because of the recurring need to revise textbooks we keep a continuing file of newspaper and periodical clippings, in addition to other materials, on the various subjects in which we are interested. Since these include government, the relations between government and business, and public administration, the combined area is a large one. As *The New York Times* is a good source of current information and of clues to other sources, we clip it regularly. Hence when we went to Turkey we did not discontinue our subscription and by the time we returned to the States the stack of unopened newspapers dating back fifteen months and piled in the upstairs study at the farm looked like a cord of wood. We loaded them in the jeep wagon and took them to Northfield with us.

I got down to the job of reading and clipping them as soon as we were settled and it took me three months to complete the job. At first it seemed a pretty tedious occupation but soon it became so interesting I couldn't keep away from it. Here was modern history in a capsule. Among other developments, Senator McCarthy's investigation of the Army and then the censure hearings on the Senator himself occupied pages of space every day. But they were safely in the past, I knew how they had come out, and my blood pressure stayed down.

To sit at my desk for hours at a time each day while outside the window the season changed from blustering, whirling, white winter to burgeoning, wet, green spring, was equally interesting. When spring came in Northfield it was with as much beauty in one place as I've ever seen. The winds dropped to breezes that melted the snow, midday was sunny on the back porch and I took my lunch out there, the mourning doves began to call, and buds appeared where only a little while ago the branches had been stiff with ice and snow.

On the campus at Carleton the lovely landscaping includes a stream, several ponds, and many fruit trees and flowering shrubs, as well as several acres of lilacs of every variety that will grow at that latitude. When the boys and girls of Carleton began to lie on the grass between classes, to wander around hand in hand, and to lose themselves among the lilacs, then we knew that winter had gone. With the balmy weather we moved our bed to the sleeping porch. To wake and watch the early morning sunshine through the thick foliage of trees that hugged the porch was a good way to start the day.

It was at about this time that my husband was asked to join the faculty of New York University as head of the government department. Although to return to a permanent appointment would mean a radical change in our way of life, we had no difficulty in deciding to accept the offer. We had had eight years of much living at home and much writing, both of which had been primary objectives when we chose the freedom to starve, if that was what it was to be. Indeed, far from starving, we had not only eaten better than ever from the produce of our own land but had also eaten widely and marvelously of the foods of a number of different nations and cultures—and enjoyed all of it.

Nevertheless, a period of withdrawal eventually generates a desire to return to active duty, and it was so with us. My husband accepted the NYU appointment and we made our plans accordingly. When the semester closed at Carleton we packed the car almost to the roof, slid a bicycle in on top of the load on one side and the boy on the other, and set out for home.

At the farm the house was quickly opened, the garden planted, and arrangements made for a building project we had long desired. This was a proper study, to be erected above the retaining wall beyond the woodshed. Big windows would look out over the garden and the pond. The view would also include the young evergreens that my husband had so lovingly set out on the crest of the hill above the pastures and beyond. Planted as seedlings, these trees were now better than thirty feet high and made a fine showing on the skyline to the west of the homestead.

Our carpenter-stonemason-electrician neighbor agreed to build the study with his brother and my husband as helpers. I drew the plans, we used lumber salvaged from the house on the upper place, and stone for the chimney and fireplace from the foundations of an old sugar house. The inside panelling was of pine cut from our own trees and sawed and finished at a local mill. Proportions were judged by the eye or, in the case of the mantelpiece, by the elbow, and turned out all right.

All summer the work on the study went forward and by September it was done. We had begun to use it even before that. As soon as the roof was on it provided a kind of pavilion for picnics and at least twice for entertaining. Thanks to President Eisenhower, this function was much simplified for us that summer. A farm rally at Rutland had been planned at which the President, then in the vicinity of Vermont, would be a guest. A friend of ours at the Aggie school was asked to put on a chicken barbecue, at which he is expert. Plans were made to feed ten thousand people and when only six thousand showed up, our friend was left with a great many barbecued chickens on hand. He stored them in a freeze locker and then sold them as the opportunity offered. We took fifty for our own freezer and had only to heat them over a picnic grill or in the oven to have a delicious meal. Served with a big green salad, plenty of red wine (yes, red), and homemade bread, this kind of entertaining was easy on guests and hostess alike. Each summer since then our friend has barbecued a few extra chickens for us at the various functions at which he serves and we always have them on hand.

* * *

Where a previous summer had seen the end of the beef barbecue that nearly became an annual event, this summer saw the end of another project, one we had initiated several years before and which finally misfired, much to our regret.

In the fall of 1950 when Davis was four and there were four other children on the farm, we had bought a young Welsh pony foal, red and white with bright eyes and perky ears, independent in temperament, and only just weaned. My idea had been that the children and the pony would grow up together and be pals. What I overlooked was that the pony would grow up much faster than the children and become adept and adult while they remained kids—smart but lacking in experience. In addition, he was an unusually intelligent animal and quickly learned how to get his way with everyone on the farm except me, the reason for the exception being that I had once had a pony of my own plus a mother who, among other things, was a horsewoman. But this pony gave me such a hard time that I repeatedly lost my courage about the whole project.

On the other hand, he was one of the most attractive and responsive little demons in the world and we loved him dearly. He could unlatch the barn door and let himself in to where the feed bin was kept and unless the cover was well secured, would push it aside with his nose and gorge himself. He could take the bars down from any gateway where they were not nailed or tied with a stout rope, simply by getting his neck under a bar and then lifting and working it sideways until one end was out of its slot in the fencepost. He could always pull away at will from any child leading him to water and then, holding his head to one side so as not to trip on the rope, run up and down the road, head and tail up and stepping high.

We named him Jabez—Jabe for short—and with the help of the man from whom we bought him, I started to train him when he was a year old. But here was another miscalculation. Training a horse is something that must be constant, and with my many absences from the farm, Jabe's training was constantly interrupted. With a biting harness I broke him to the bridle and to drive. But when I came to ride him a year later I discovered one of his more distressing habits: going along quietly, suddenly he would see a tiger or a dragon in the bushes along the roadside and in a single lightning and sustained motion he would stop-jump-to-one-side-turn-and-head-for-home at a full gallop. As he turned I would be half out of the saddle, and only my childhood handling of a similar beast with a similarly distorted sense of fun kept me from leaving it altogether.

The first time Jabe pulled this trick on me I was riding him bareback and lost control of him for a moment as he dashed down the hill toward home. As I struggled to stay aboard I had a sudden clear realization—like the reputed flash in the consciousness of a drowning man—that at my age my bones were no longer of the young-sapling quality described in my seventh-grade physiology textbook as being character- istic of the bones of the young. Indeed, I suspected that my bones were now highly brittle and that it would do me no good at all to slide off that pony's heaving back, as I had every desire to do.

After two or three summers of this kind of nonsense, we turned Jabe over to a professional horse trainer when we returned from Minnesota, and he did a fine job on him. He also did a fine job on Davis and in a short time taught him the fundamentals of riding according to Hoyle. (My own system was merely to get on and stay on, with due attention to hands and posture, but today it seems that this field too has been invaded by professional specialization.) With this start, experience for boy and pony would have to be more gradually acquired. So, full of hope and minus a considerable fee, we brought Jabe home, set up an equitation ring at the foot of the garden, and prepared to continue training.

Here yet another fatal flaw appeared in my calculations. The professional trainer had taught Jabe his manners all right, but had confined him to a ring. And so long as Jabe was handled in a ring he did very well. Also, he was a gentle animal when he chose, tame and playful, the kind that goes quickly to the heart of one who likes horses, and we do. But the first time I tried him again on the road he saw not only tigers and dragons but hobgoblins as well; although never, strangely enough, on the way home—only on the outward road. And again I had the uncomfortable experience of never being quite sure when he would let his imagination—or his malice—get the better of his manners. Davis also had trouble with him and was even less prepared than I to cope with him.

More than once when I was a child learning to ride, Mom had warned me, "Never trust a horse." Trying to get Jabe to behave, I kept remembering this advice. The difference between Jabe and Mom's girlhood grey was that Jabe had no spark of meanness in him, just an excess of intelligence, high spirits, and a bit of the devil. Plenty of daily exercise might have cured him but I didn't have the time for it and the kids didn't have the ability.

I kept hoping for some way out of the impasse, and finally consulted my philosopher-blacksmith friend, as we always did when in difficulty with some farm project. Lew listened carefully to my troubles and then suggested that if Jabe could be ridden regularly with other horses on the road he might learn road manners; at a certain girls' camp in the vicinity the director was a professional horseman and might take Jabe on for me. It was worth a try. I called at the camp and the director was glad to cooperate. He would call for Jabe that week and ride him back to camp.

On the appointed day the director and five or six of his riders rode in at the farm. Jabe, who was tethered on the back lawn, pricked up his ears and began to take an interest. He always became excited at the approach of his own kind. I introduced him to the camp director who liked his looks at once. Everybody did. I put a bridle on him but the director refused a saddle.

By this time Jabe had got the general idea that he was

to figure in the current proceedings and became very alert indeed. The other riders set off up the road, the camp director mounted Jabe and prepared to follow, and Jabe decided that nothing on earth could induce him to leave the place. He reared and plunged for a few minutes, almost throwing himself but not his rider who had a good seat. Jabe then set his legs at a backward angle, dug his heels in, and refused to move at all. I handed the director a branch off a young maple in lieu of a crop, Jabe gave it one glance and took off after the other horses at a mad gallop up the hill.

Ten minutes later the other riders had reversed their course and were coming back down the hill followed by the camp director leading Jabe. This pony, he said, was not a suitable animal for a girls' camp. We could only agree. So Jabe went back to his tether on the lawn, the riders departed, and we put an ad in the local paper offering one pony for sale.

A few days later a young man and his wife and two small children drove up to the farm and asked about the pony. My first question was, Can the children ride? Yes, they could. The family owned two Morgan horses and wanted a pony for the children.

Jabe was staked out near the garden and acknowledged introductions in his most charming manner. He nuzzled the children and they loved him. We got out the saddle and bridle and he was ridden in the ring, performing admirably even for the children whom I could see were not exactly experienced riders. I explained about his behavior on the road. The father of the family then mounted him bareback and took him up the road a piece, noting "a certain wilfulness," as he put it. When the father explained, however, that he was a former cavalry officer I received that information with relief;

surely so experienced a horseman would know how to handle this situation.

As for the other members of the family, it was a case of love at first sight. We agreed on a price. They would fetch Jabe in a few days. And so they did. The mother was to ride him the twenty-five miles from our place to theirs. I figured that after a workout of that length Jabe would be in no condition to show much excitement on meeting the two Morgans —at first, anyhow—even though one of them was a mare. Jabe had been duly gelded and in theory, at least, should have had no interest in mares. But the fact was, he did.

I watched him and his gentle rider and new owner go off down the hill at a quiet pace, Jabe waggling his behind in a rather tentative way that seemed to suggest he had not quite made up his mind about this person now on his back. But he would. I could imagine him thinking to himself, in that clever little mind of his and a gentle look in his eyes:

"I wonder how good a rider she is. I'll get to know her a little better before I find out."

We nearly wept to see him go, we were so fond of the little demon. But my husband drove right to town to deposit the check before Jabe betrayed his true colors and his new owners changed their minds. It was just a little over a year later that I saw an ad in the paper offering for sale a red-and-white Welsh pony, suitable for a child over ten years of age. If this was Jabe, it was the last I heard of our little friend and I often wonder what has happened to him.

*   *   *

Another job that summer was to find suitable, more or less permanent living quarters for the family in New York. As my husband was going back into academic harness in September, we'd have to be settled before that and have Davis entered in a new school.

We had decided as a matter of policy to live in the city, ruling out the suburbs because of the wear and tear of commutation on the head of the family. We would spend vacations on the farm, which was always home to Davis (to whom by contrast, New York was "that old garbage pail") as it was to us, and our legal residence would remain Vermont. We needed a minimum of four rooms and five would be better. With a family made up two-thirds of men folk and one of them a growing boy accustomed to woodsheds, pastures, and forests for his playground, ample living space seemed not only desirable but indispensable.

So one day in June I accompanied my husband to New York and we started looking for an apartment in the Washington Square area. Before noon we had found what we wanted in Brooklyn Heights: a big cooperative with a wide view of the harbor extending from Brooklyn Bridge down through the Narrows. My husband had once promised me—half joking, no doubt—that if I found an apartment with a harbor view he would take me abroad again. This was it.

Furnishing it was even easier than finding it because we still had Mom's house full of furniture: a few old family pieces, some of which I had cut my teeth on, plus pieces that Mom had collected in the course of her travels and at auctions. So one day I packed a picnic lunch, took a blueprint of the new apartment, and drove down to Mom's Place. I set a card table and a lawn chair under the big butternut tree, and with the plans, went to work and furnished the new place with what was in the house beside me, going in to look at a piece now and then if I needed to. It was a lovely quiet day and somehow the spirit of the independent lady who had owned the place seemed very near and helpful and maybe even a little amused. I ate my lunch without stopping work, and by the end of the afternoon I knew how the Brooklyn place would look down to the last lamp.

What furniture I didn't want was just plain junk, as Mom would have been the first to acknowledge, and none of it was anything she had ever cared for in any special way. So we arranged to hold an auction of our own. It was duly announced for a certain day which, however, proved to be the one on which Hurricane Diane, having devastated parts of Connecticut and Massachusetts, flipped her tail over Vermont as well. But neither wind nor rain seemed to reduce the size of the crowd that came to bid on this and that. A friend, wise in the ways of auction attenders, allayed my early fears in the matter of prospective buyers by commenting that auctions, fires, and murder trials will always draw a crowd irrespective of weather or other obstacles.

"A man will bid on and pay good money," he said, "for a box of junk that he wouldn't stop his car to pick up if he saw it on the side of the road."

And so it proved. Out of mostly junk and despite the storm (we were able to move the crowd inside the studio during the worst of it) we netted a neat sum. Even better, I and other members of the family had taken advantage of the opportunity to get rid of some junk of our own that had accumulated from our own injudicious bidding at other auctions and had either never needed, needed no longer, or already replaced with other auction loot.

I don't like to pack and move out of a place but I do like

to unpack and move into one. In Brooklyn I did the job with the help of a sister but mostly alone. Men are occasionally eager to help at such times but often prove less than useful. My husband had to attend a conference in Chicago and I think he was as relieved as I was. So for a week I worked, happily sorting, arranging, setting up the kitchen and closets and bureau drawers, following the plans I had made under the butternut tree.

When all was ready the family joined me and we settled into our new quarters like an apple in its skin. The space inside (eight rooms) was enhanced by the broad harbor view outside that was a constant enchantment. A bright sunrise or a cold grey dawn, a balmy blue day and smooth water, or a battering wind that made the windows rattle, a quiet summer dusk or a winter snowstorm that half obscured the skyscrapers of lower Manhattan, a flaming sunset behind the Statue of Liberty or a bleak end of the day—the variations kept us going to the windows in the midst of other occupations to see what was happening.

Then there was the constant movement in the harbor that gave the view from our windows yet another dimension. Passenger ships, naval vessels (Brooklyn Navy Yard is just up the river), tankers, tugs, freighters, barges, lighters, oilers, ferries, launches, fishing boats, and even an occasional sailing vessel filled the harbor with a constant coming and going beneath our windows.

A moment of magic occurs at dusk at the end of a winter afternoon. Since daylight fails before closing time in the offices on lower Manhattan, the lights in the massed buildings there come on early. Then a cool mist appears over the East River, adding distance and increasing the feeling, common in

Brooklyn and New York alike, that in many ways the two cities are worlds apart. After a brief moment of suspended time between day and night, darkness comes on, the mist clears, and the lights of New York stand out clearly. Ships and tugs go by, only their lights visible. On the East River Drive a line of moving headlights going south is part of a pattern of motion that includes a higher line of lights on Brooklyn Bridge going east. While the cleaning women are at work the office buildings of Manhattan are brightly lit, but on weekends they are mostly dim. Often one window high in a deserted office tower will be bright when it seems it should be dark—some poor man (it could hardly be a woman) overly concerned with his economic life. We came to think of him as Mr. Stomach Ulcer.

*   *   *

Were we back in harness now, or were we not? What about those ocean liners we could see, without even getting out of bed, as they moved deliberately up the harbor in the early morning light? Worse, we could see them sail forth again, usually around lunchtime or in the late afternoon against a sunset, headed for who knew what high adventure. And at a line of docks immediately below our windows, freighters from all over the world tied up to exchange cargo.

My husband's appointment at the university was a permanent one. We quickly formed new ties in a community as congenial as any in New York, in a location that could hardly be more beautiful and remain urban. The return to full-time academic work was rewarding. We still had the farm. Everything was fine, in fact. But we weren't exactly resigned to it.

CHAPTER 14

It's Still Fun

ON A BRIGHT COLD JANUARY DAY, FOURTEEN YEARS AFTER OUR declaration of personal independence and six years after our return to a permanent academic appointment, I sit here in the study at Scrivelsby and look out the big windows to the skyline where my husband's 100 acres of pines, only seedlings a few years ago, are now a dark green forest of young trees against the heavy snow. This book was started during a sojourn in London, most of it was written in Brooklyn Heights, and it seems fitting now that it should be topped off in the study on the farm. Big logs are burning in the fireplace, and outside the sun is shining on the snow to make one of those white and blue and gold days that are the hallmark of winter in Vermont. In here I can't hear them but if I were to step outside for a moment I know I'd hear the chickadees chattering where they winter on the knoll just beyond the study.

This is a kind of transitional period in the family adventure in freedom. My husband has taken a year's leave of absence from the University. (Remember? The last time we did that, it turned out to be permanent.) He is writing another book and the first draft is nearly done. In a couple of weeks we're leaving for three months abroad, to hole up somewhere on a Swiss mountainside to write the second draft in different and congenial surroundings. We have found this to be a good way to write and always manage to do it at foundation expense.

*   *   *

Since this is a transition, perhaps it is also the place to try to figure out what we have gained by freedom, and to cast a controlled glance ahead to see what just possibly lies there. I say a "controlled" glance because if what seems to beckon shouldn't work out just the way we'd like it to, there would be quite a disappointment. Don't count your chickens, etc.

Well, so far as the present is concerned, I think we now know a little more about the non-romantic, practical aspects of freedom than we did when we left Evanston. The essence of it is this: Freedom is more a matter of clearing your time to do something you want to do than it is getting away from restraints or from institutions, as is more often considered to be the case. There is freedom of a sort even in a large university, though of a different quality from the kind we know when we are on our own at Scrivelsby. The reason, of course, is that to cope with the trammels of the institution is harder than to cope with the demands of a simple rural setting.

Thus, on a recent summer, we rented a house on the Channel Island of Alderney to write the final draft of the book then in process. By this time it was largely my job, and in such a lovely place it seemed senseless to spend the whole of every day in the study. So I got up at 4:45 each morning, had a delightfully quiet breakfast in the kitchen, and by 5:30 was at work. Two hours later a neighbor ran in to get breakfast for the family, I joined them for a second one myself, and went back to the study where my husband joined me for his part of the work, and by noon we were done for the day. Then picnics on the beaches, swimming in the clear (and rather cold) water, walking along the cliffs and through fields of wild flowers including acres of heather in bloom, exploring the remains of fortifications left from the German occupation during the war, getting to know something of the local people and their habits—all this was largely a matter of being free to organize one's time as the need required.

To my husband, freedom is a feeling of inner contentment that comes from a way of life to which he is suited. Scrivelsby is both symbolically and actually the way of life that he prefers for creative work. His area of professional and writing interest has long been: how to keep the human spirit and the initiative and enterprise associated with individualism alive and vigorous when institiutions become, as apparently they must, big, formal, bureaucratic, and hidebound.

For him also, the best way of acquiring first-hand insights, plus the time to reflect and possibly break new ground in his professional field, is through a series of withdrawals and returns of the sort described by Arnold Toynbee, of the sort that governed our decision in 1955 to return to full-time teaching. There is no substitute for active participation in the mainstream of life in a going society, but if one is not to become sucked in and surrounded and absorbed by the institutional aspects of it, thus losing objectivity and the ability to innovate, then one must occasionally leave it in order—as my husband would say—to secure balance.

This is where Scrivelsby comes in. Independence would have been harder for us had we not, through all these years of coming and going, had a home to which to return after each sortie, a place to keep our chattels, animals, trees, books, files, and papers. (Here, even, is the cemetery in which we expect to be buried.) It seems almost as though a part of us stays behind every time we leave the place, acting as a kind of guardian angel during our absences and ready to welcome us back. We've always been able to return here to lick our wounds, if any; to plan new ventures; or decide to remain for good if we want to. On these 360 acres, amid the ceaseless activity of a going farm operation, we find the simplicity that helps to counteract the institutional and emotional complexities man makes for himself and his fellows.

For my part, freedom has meant all this and something more, for in addition to other occupations I am also a housewife in a servantless era. Consequently I've had to work out some special problems for myself. I used to be a perfectionist, for example, which is a hard thing for anyone to live with. Now I am a perfectionist only in the work I like to do. My daily round follows a number of guidelines which, to me at least, make sense. Thus, my Vermont neighbors "let the horse bother" and now so do I. A man I once worked for, when confronted with a complicated situation, generally "let nature take its course" and I saw how easily that could be done. A lady of much wisdom believes one should "let people make their own decisions," a rule that relieves me of much stewing over what is none of my business. In my housekeeping

I follow the rule of my doctor-sister to "keep it simple" and my own discovery that "if it's neat it's enough." But if something must be done carefully, then according to my brother, "it's the corners that count."

By following these guidelines I've tried to free my time for the many things I like to do. Thus I am presently writing a book. Last year I revised a textbook which was an excuse to spend long hours each day in the study. I am cultivating a green thumb and wish my mother were still around to see the garden because she tried so hard to show me how much pleasure lies in this area. I enjoy using my hands at occupations like refinishing old furniture and hooking rug, and I should like to learn to weave. Increasingly I enjoy reading and the luxury of having time for it. I know no greater pleasure, after a day's work, than to sit with a book, my feet up, and a tea-tray beside me, even if I have to put the tray there myself.

As the only one of our children to go the full course with us, Davis also has enjoyed aspects of freedom that a more conventional upbringing might have denied him. There is, for example, the incomparable asset of the woodshed, not as a traditional place of juvenile correction but as one where children can exercise their minds and bodies, release their energies, use their imaginations, their inventiveness, their urge to experiment, to make things. Watching children playing (if that is the right word) on the streets of Brooklyn, I have wondered how different might be their future social attitudes and usefulness if they had had the advantages of a woodshed full of tools, nails, nuts and bolts, odds and ends of lumber, old iron, tin, paint, putty, flower pots, oil cans, a wheelbarrow, a stepladder, a pair of sawhorses, a mess of ropes, chains, and wire, a hose, and stacks of firewood with

226

which a child may build a farm or a fortress. Davis has had all these satisfactions and I think he is easier to live with because of them.

In addition, because of our travels he has attended many schools, being now in his tenth. Some would call this a disaster but I believe that in his case, at least, it has been an asset (partly, perhaps, because he makes friends easily). He entered school at five instead of six but has never lost a year nor failed a subject, and now in his high-school years he is consistently on honors. He is also a cross-country runner and knows all about organized baseball, football, basketball, golf, and hockey. By reason of the periodic need to adjust to a new school he has acquired poise, independence, and a sense of discrimination. When he was not yet twelve, for example, he insisted on going to England ahead of us, alone by ship (though he had never been on one before) in mid-January when the seas were bound to be rough. He didn't want to miss the first part of the new school term in England, he said; we suspected that an urge for adventure was the real motive. He argued that Mark, who was then in the Air Force and stationed in London, could meet him. With the consent of the Cunard Line, we let him go. On a cold windy day we put him aboard the *Parthia*, and after inspecting the ship with us and allowing me to unpack his bags, he nearly threw us off.

"You might as well go now," he told us. And we did.

Not without understandable parental misgivings, to be sure, but we kept them to ourselves. Mark met him at Liverpool, took him to London, bought him his school outfit, and put him on the train for Devon. By the time we caught up with him six weeks later he was very, very glad to see us. He had hated the trip because of almost constant seasickness (I'm glad I didn't know about it at the time), but not because of being alone. Although he was the only American at the boarding school, he settled into it like an old hand and regards it as one of the best he has ever attended. He should know.

For all of us, freedom has meant withdrawal from time to time but it has never been an escape. Under modern conditions, a desire to escape seems often enough to be justified, but it is nevertheless a negative action, not a positive one. A desire for the kind of freedom we have is positive, and hedonistic in the sense that we try to do what we want to do; but also it inspires and challenges and hence produces a satisfying feeling of accomplishment without tension or strain or pressure except of the kind that gets things done.

Far from being a life of ease and vegetation, freedom may mean working harder than you ever worked before. But because it's what you like and want to do, nothing about it is burdensome. Not even early morning barn chores in winter, or playing midwife to a sow, or getting out of a warm bed to tend fires in the night, or scrubbing the kitchen floor more often than seems reasonable because the menfolk pick up assorted kinds of barn debris on their boots and despite repeated and pointed comment, seldom do a complete job of decontamination. Or, for the men, the jobs of heavy garden work, putting on storm windows, and working in the woods with the temperature at zero or below in order to keep up the wood supply for the three or four fires that substitute for central heating, their appetites ravenous when the mercury seems to be stuck at the bottom of the thermometer.

On the intellectual side is our writing. My husband once

remarked that a colleague was taking a sabbatical in order
to write a book.

"Do you think he'll write it?" I asked.

"No," he said.

"Why not? Doesn't he have a book in him?"

"Oh yes, he has a book in him, all right," said my husband,
"but he doesn't have the hormones."

I laughed. I understood him but would have been hard put
to it to explain just what the term "hormones" meant in the
context of authorship. Being intrigued with a description
so apt and yet so elusive, I have thought about it a good deal.
The hormones of authorship, I conclude, are the ability to
sit down and actually do a job of writing. They are the link
between thought and manuscript, the active determination of
an author to write what he has decided to write.

If this is a correct analysis, then between us my husband
and I must be well supplied with the right kind of hormones
because in fourteen years that have included trade books,
textbooks, and rewrites for new editions, we have produced
something like twelve books, which isn't too bad when one
considers all the teaching, traveling, farming, and legislating
that we also accomplished. It seems unlikely that so much
writing could have been done along with a full-time university
schedule, without the chance not only to spend consecutive
uninterrupted hours in the study, but also the opportunity to
leave it in order to renew oneself by working in the woods,
or hoeing in the garden, or scything long grass along the
edges of the homestead, or just splitting and piling wood.
We both find regular exercise to be an indispensable accompaniment of authorship.

We have also learned that that fearful disaster, the Long

Winter Evening, is a myth. The need to face up to such a catastrophe is what seems mostly to worry our city friends who ask us about our way of life at Scrivelsby. What in the world do we do after dinner and the long hours drag through the evening before the open fire in the living room? What indeed? All we do is relax, watch the fire, talk a bit, sew, read, listen to music, hook rug, smoke a pipe. I had heard a good deal about the reputed dreariness of these hours of the day on the farm so I did some research on the subject. Everyone in the neighborhood whom I have questioned has heard of long winter evenings, but no one has ever seen one. The fact is that in the country—winter and summer alike—evenings, and days too, for that matter, are never long enough for all the delightful things one would like to do.

Nor from the financial standpoint do we have any complaints. We have improved the farm, both land and buildings; put the older children through college and one of them through graduate school; and entered Davis in private schools when necessary. About half our income during the eight-year period of freedom came from book royalties and the other half from visiting professorships and the United-Nations assignment. The farm operation was and always has been a break-even proposition. We supply the cows; the farm operator contributes his know-how and his labor; and as he gets most of the income, he has an incentive to produce as only an owner-operator can. But we get the increase in the herd and carry on the forestry operation.

The real economy, however, is in minimizing expenses compared with living in the city. We pay no rent, and heat is supplied by our own labor. Foodstuffs and meat, except for the usual staples, are produced on the farm. An average grocery bill may be $40 a month compared with $150 or more in the city. Real estate taxes, insurance, and maintenance may cost us $600 a year compared with a city rent of $3600. Hence, doing most of our own work and being gluttons for it, almost automatically we have saved money for education and retirement.

So far from learning what it's like to starve, therefore, we have learned instead what it's like to have a great plenty of that which, for us, constitutes the good life: Freedom from debt. Freedom from the crashing bore of social occasions arranged from a sense of duty. Time saved by not having to drive to work, ride a subway, or wait for appointments. Heating the house and cooking with wood cut by ourselves (or a neighbor) from our own forest. Drinking whole milk that has been spared the indignities of pasteurization because it comes from our own certified herd. Going to the garden with a basket on the arm to pick dinner vegetables just before time to prepare them for the pot. Making bread and pie, and broiling meat over live coals in the wood-burning range instead of under a controlled gas flame or electrical unit. Hanging the family wash on a sunny breezy day, knowing that it won't be sooted over in half an hour or so. Planting pines and potatoes and peonies. Listening while still in bed to the medley of bird songs at dawn on a spring morning (I once heard a bird clear his throat and try three times before he got the right pitch). Contemplating an apple tree in full bloom just outside the window. Watching deer digging for frozen apples under the snow in the moonlight under the same tree on a winter night (nothing funnier than watching a doe at close range, her mouth full of frozen apple, trying to crush the wretched thing). Watching the antics of little pigs and puppies and kittens and calves. Picking wild strawberries and raspberries and blackberries and eating them with lots of our own fresh cream or making jam to be enjoyed at a winter breakfast when the snow is deep and shining beyond the windows and the kitchen is full of the good smells of firewood, sausage, toast, and coffee. Bringing in the winter vegetables and putting down salt pork and corned beef and eggs. Filling the woodshed with a dozen or more cords of seasoned logs and chunks—no finer sight! Watching the leaves turn the hillsides crimson and gold, and then blow off to reveal the fine etchings of bare trees against a bare background. Listening to the silence of lightly falling snow or watching it on a stormy night blowing wildly in the light from the window of a room where the open fire burns brightly. Then waking in the morning to find a world that is white and blue and gold, with the kind of crispness that accompanies a temperature of 10 degrees below zero—the kind of weather that stimulates the body and clears the brain.

There have been several occasions in the past two or three years when we have been tempted to declare our freedom again, for the lure of life at Scrivelsby is always strong. Like the Angel Gabriel about to sound his trumpet in the play "Green Pastures," however, something has told us to "Hold it!" and we have. But for how long? The time may come when we shall no longer be content to "hold it." Indeed, we can see the day.

*   *   *

And now the day has come! Less than a year since this manuscript was finished, at the end of the current semester at the university, a jeep and rented trailer loaded with the books, papers, typewriters, kitchen ware, and house plants needed in temporary winter quarters in the city, will, with me at the wheel, head for the north country, there to remain except for what we hope will in the future be only minor sorties. No more than last time is our plan in any sense a retirement; just a chance to simplify our life again and clear the decks for the work that lies ahead.

LB1782 .D5   010101 000
Dimock, Gladys Gouverneur
A home of our own.

0 2002 0048766 4

YORK COLLEGE OF PENNSYLVANIA 17403

LB
1782
.D5
DIMOCK
HOME OF OUR OWN

20969

DISCARDED